How to Use Limited Liability Companies and Limited Partnerships

Second Edition

Garrett Sutton, Esq.

A SuccessDNA® Publication

A SuccessDNA Nonfiction Book

Editor: Cindie Geddes
Page design: Megan Hughes, Eh? Clerical Services Inc.
Cover design: Tammy Ackerman, MeshCreative

SuccessDNA, Inc.

Printed in the United States of America
10 9 8 7 6 5 4 3 2 1

Library of Congress Control No: 2001-130679
ISBN No. 0-9713549-01

This publication is designed to provide general information regarding the subject matter covered. Because each individual's legal, tax, and financial situation is different, specific advice should be tailored to the particular circumstances. For this reason, the reader is advised to consult with his or her own attorney, accountant and/or other advisor regarding that individual's specific situation. The author has taken reasonable precautions in the preparation of this book and believes that the information presented in the book is accurate as of the date it was written. However, neither the author nor the publisher assume any responsibility for any errors or omissions. The author and publisher specifically disclaim any liability resulting from the use or application of the information contained in this book, and the information is not intended to serve as legal, tax, or other financial advice related to individual situations.

For Mom and Dad

Thanks for everything.

Contents

How to Use Limited Liability Companies and Limited Partnerships

Second Edition

Acknowledgements

It is with great appreciation that I acknowledge the efforts of friends and colleagues in the preparation of this book. First, to Megan Hughes and Robert Paul Turner, for their efforts, advice and guidance in the shaping of the manuscript. The professional input of two CPA's, Mike Bosma of Grant Thornton and Mel Williams, of Cupit, Milligan, Ogden & Williams, both located in Reno, Nevada, has been invaluable. As well, the advice of Jack Hanifan, Esq., on estate planning matters and Craig Demetras, Esq., on bankruptcy and divorce matters, also both from Reno, has been valued.

For the second edition of *How to Use Limited Liability Companies and Limited Partnerships*, I would like to acknowledge the invaluable assistance of Matthew Dearing.

Also, thanks are offered to my wife and children, Jenny, Teddy, Emily and Sarah for their patience as this book was being written.

Introduction

Congratulations. You are about to learn powerful legal strategies used by the rich for generations to protect their assets and operate their businesses. By reading this book, you will come to understand the concepts necessary to establish a customized strategy for the protection of your business and personal assets and to create your own legal defense against the improper threats and claims of would-be creditors. You will learn when and how to use Limited Liability Companies and Limited Partnerships both in specific situations and in general business scenarios. And you will learn a mantra and attitude that the rich have successfully used for hundreds of years – protect and grow. How to protect and grow your assets through the strategic use of Limited Liability Companies, Limited Partnerships or Corporations is one of the greatest skills you can acquire.

The journey begins with a consideration of the entities you can use to your maximum advantage.

Chapter One
Entity Selection

This book is designed to explain how and when to use two of the most popular and powerful business entities available today. As you go through the book you will learn that both Limited Partnerships (LPs) and Limited Liability Companies (LLCs) offer the advantages of:

- Limited liability
- Protection from creditors
- Retained management control
- Family wealth transfers
- Transfer restrictions
- Flow Through Taxation
- Flexibility

The question of when to use either an LP or an LLC will be discussed first in this chapter where we will review scenarios for each entity. Later chapters employ a question and answer approach as well as scenarios to deal with such issues as management, taxation and specialized uses for each entity.

It is important to note that there are two separate and distinct uses of the LP and LLC. One use is for the operation of a business and the other is for the holding of assets. In some cases the two uses are accomplished by one entity. LPs and LLCs, as well as General Partnerships, Corporations and Sole Proprietorships, have been used for either purpose. Throughout this book, by distinguishing between the two uses – business operations and asset holdings – the intent is to arrive at the best possible entity selection for your particular purpose.

Using Advisors

As we go through the chapters there will be instances where I suggest you consult with your professional advisor – be it a lawyer, accountant or financial planner. In other books

I have written, some readers have been upset by these references, their concern being why pay for a book that directs them to a high-priced professional.

My answer to this is three-fold. First, by reading this book you will become well educated in the field. You will either know with certainty – or have a very good idea – on how to start. By not requiring your professional to educate you on basic business concepts (i.e., types of entities, flow-through taxation issues, preliminary estate planning concepts and basic business skills), you have already saved hundreds, if not thousands, of dollars in consultation fees. By being able to walk into a professional's office with a strategy and a set of specific questions to which you couldn't find an answer or didn't quite understand, you will be able to get right to the heart of the matter, saving time and money. Your professional can play devil's advocate with your strategy or suggest certain fine-tuning elements to enhance it, meaning that the consulting fee you wind up paying has a far greater value than if you walked in off the street cold, with little or no idea on how to begin capturing your dream. In other words, use your professional to maximize your strategy.

Secondly, the laws in the areas we are covering can be broad and sometimes complex. One book cannot cover every nuance. By giving you a heads-up on the fundamentals of a certain topic, your advisor can instead concentrate their time on the technical details and most tax-beneficial strategy for you. By focusing their effort on the technicalities, they may be able to refine your strategy in a manner that will save you several thousand dollars in your business. And that's how you should look at your accountant or lawyer – from a cost benefit analysis approach. Should you spend $750 on an accountant to save $5,000? It's your choice. Because certain laws and tax regulations are downright and annoyingly complex, it is really not worth your time to deal with them. You likely have a business to run and a family to raise. You don't need to be spending your weekends learning the arcania of the recapture rules for depreciable assets. Pay someone who does it for a living to do it for you. And remember, while our laws can be complex, in complexity comes advantage. Working with a professional to take advantage of complexity can be very worthwhile. The rich have done so for a very long time.

The third part of my answer is that by reading this book you will be better able to judge your advisor's capabilities. You don't want to retain or continue with just any professional. You have the right to deal with the professional with whom you are most comfortable and in whom you have the most confidence. If the lawyer or accountant you are interviewing tells you to put rental property into a C Corporation, you will know to get up and walk out. That knowledge alone can also save you thousands of dollars in the long run.

Types of Entities

The best way to select the entity most suited to your use is to compare it to other available entities. In addition to LPs and LLCs, the traditional means of doing business or holding assets have been Sole Proprietorships, General Partnerships, C Corporations and S Corporations. We shall compare the advantages and disadvantages of each.

As a frame of reference for making your selection, it is important to clarify your strategy during the planning process. To that end, the following checklist should be considered:

1. The nature of the business to be operated.
2. The nature of the asset to be held.
3. Protection of family assets and investments.
4. Management control.
5. The number of owners involved.
6. Estate planning and gifting of assets.
7. Succession of children and other family members to management.
8. Avoiding family disputes.
9. Who may legally obligate the business.
10. Flexibility of decisions making.
11. The need for start-up funding.

12. Taxation.
13. Effect upon an owner's death or departure.
14. Segregation of assets and investments.
15. Privacy of ownership.

These and other issues will become apparent as we review your choices. And, if after reading this book you still aren't sure which entity is best for your business plan, then ask your advisor to clarify what you don't understand. An attorney, accountant or other professional advisor well versed in this area should be able to answer your remaining questions so you can arrive at the best entity selection for you. If need be, you can call our office for a consultation.

Before we begin comparing LLCs, LPs and Corporations, it is important to know the language of each. While their basic structure is similar, the terms for each structural facet are different.

The Language of Corporations, Limited Liability Companies, and Limited Partnerships

Term	*Corporation*	*Limited Liability Company*	*Limited Partnership*
Owner	Shareholder	Member	General and Limited Partner
Ownership Interests	Shares or Stock	Membership Interest	Partnership Interest
Senior Management	Chairman of the board, chief executive officer (CEO); president	Manager	General Partner
Initial Filing Document (filed with the secretary of state)	Articles of Incorporation	Articles of Organization	Certificate of Limited Partnership (LP-1)
Organizational Document	Bylaws	Operating Agreement	Limited Partnership Agreement

Also, because we will be primarily discussing LLCs and LPs, and there are similarities to both, we shall use the following common terms for the review of both:

Common Term	*Limited Liability Term*	*Limited Partnership Term*
Filing Documents	Articles of Organization	Certificate of Limited Partnership
Organizational Documents	Operating Agreement	Partnership Agreement
Entity	LLC	LP
Management	Manager	General Partner
Interest Holder	Member	Limited Partner or Partner
Ownership Interests	Membership Interest	Limited Partnership Interest

We shall also use the term "better practice" to indicate a situation which may not be legally required by statute but is proper for the efficient, ethical and stress-free operation of the entity.

Before engaging in our discussion of the relevant entities it is important to see how they can relate to real-life situations. The scenarios that you and your family face right now, as you are reading this book. For that reason, we shall look at our first two case studies as a starting point for understanding.

Case Examples:

Case Number 1 – John and Liz

John and Liz have been friends since their college days together. They have both worked for large companies over the years and have grown weary of the nonsensical corporate politics and less than rapid response to marketplace changes. They want to be part of a nimble, focused and responsive organization that can take advantage of market opportunities as they present themselves. They want to maximize their prior experiences and consult with other businesses in their area of expertise.

After initially talking about starting their own business, John and Liz begin to focus on what it would really take. They consider all aspects of the issue. On the business side they read a number of business start up guides and talk to local entrepreneurs for advice. On the emotional and psychological side they read *Get Off the Couch: Seven Psychological Secrets for Success in Business,* by Kenji Sax, Ph.D., (Success DNA, 2003) and consider what effect a start-up might have on their families.

Once they feel they are mentally and financially prepared, John and Liz decide to move forward with their consulting business. They know from their readings and discussions with other business people that they need a limited liability entity, be it a Corporation or an LLC. They have raised $100,000 between them for their initial round of financing, which they believe will get them through the first year of business. It is projected that they will lose at least $70,000 in the first year of business. With the help of their accountant, they decide they should utilize a flow-through entity for tax purposes.

In terms of taxation, Sole Proprietorships, General Partnerships, Sub-Chapter S Corporations, LLCs and LPs are all flow-through tax entities. This means that, unlike C Corporations, there is no tax at the entity level. Instead, all tax obligations "flow through" the entity to the individual's personal tax return. While a greater discussion of entity taxes will be had in Chapter Four, the following chart illustrates the concept:

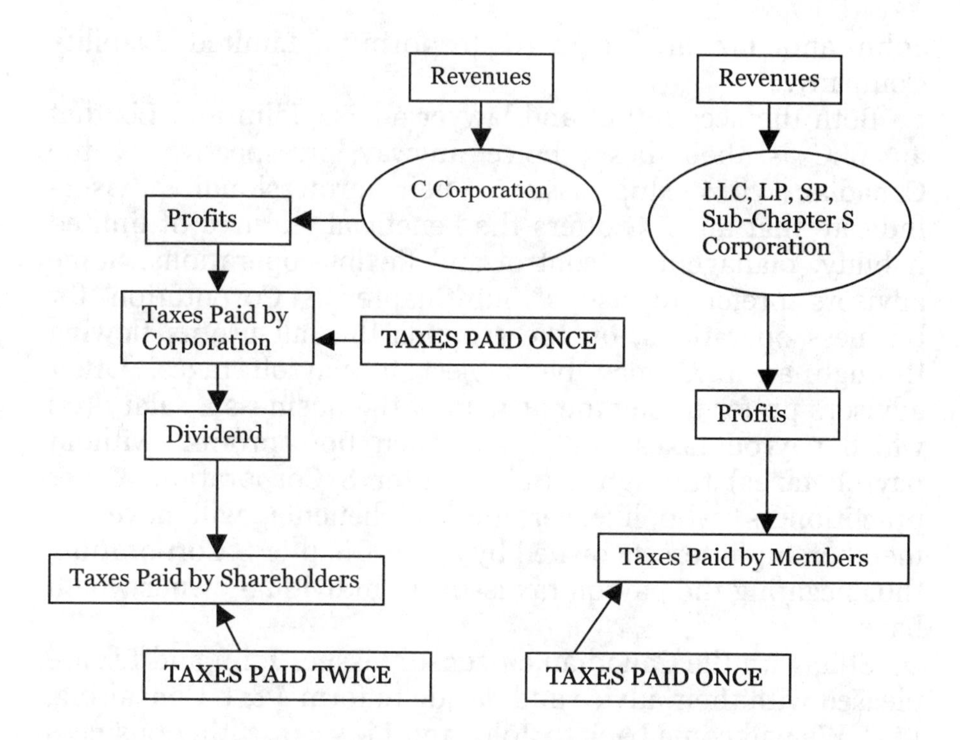

John and Liz take the advice of their accountant on the use of a flow-through entity. To be able to deduct $70,000 in losses and offset income from other sources is good tax planning for them.

Another issue arises in that John and Liz have decided that they will issue founder's equity not only to themselves but to their respective spouses as well. Liz's husband is a Canadian citizen and because he works most of the year in Vancouver, British Columbia, he is classified as a non-resident alien. This precludes them from using a Sub-Chapter S Corporation, since foreign nationals that are non-residents and not a part of the United States tax system cannot own stock in such an entity. (Foreign nationals can, however, own stock in a C Corporation, LP or LLC.)

Thus, with the desire to utilize a tax flow-through entity and the need to issue shares to a non United States citizen,

John and Liz are required to form a Limited Liability Company.

Both the accountant and lawyer advise John and Liz that an LLC is their best choice anyway, irrespective of the Canadian citizenship issue. Their professional advisors indicate that an LLC offers the beneficial features of limited liability, management control and flexible operations. Some advisors prefer to use a Sub-Chapter S Corporation for business operations, on the grounds that all profits flowing through an LLC may be subject to payroll taxes. Other advisors prefer to pay the owners of the business a salary (on which payroll taxes apply) and then flow profits (without payroll taxes) through a Sub-Chapter S Corporation. Other practitioners, who like certain LLC benefits, will have the membership interests owned by a Sub-Chapter S Corporation, thus negating the payroll tax issue an individual owner would have.

Still, with the Canadian citizenship issue, John and Liz are pleased with their advice and decide to form J & L Consulting, LLC. We will come back to John and Liz's consulting business to see how they benefit from operating as an LLC.

Case Number 2 – Mary and Gary

Mary and Gary have been married for over ten years, have three children, a dog and a mortgage. They have done well in their business careers and investments and have accumulated assets. Gary is involved in a business in which he deals with the public, which therefore means he can be sued by almost anyone for any reason. The two of them want to protect their assets. They know that if they try to shelter their assets once they have been sued, it will be considered a fraudulent conveyance and could be set aside by a court order. (We shall have a more comprehensive discussion of this concept in Chapter Fifteen.) They know that the time to protect their assets is when they are not being sued, and so they decide to move ahead with an asset protection plan. The sooner the better is their feeling.

After speaking with their accountant and lawyer they decide to form a Family Limited Partnership (FLP). A key benefit of the FLP is that it allows one party – the general partner – to maintain almost absolute control. By definition the other limited partners are limited in their management and control. They cannot tell the general partner how to run the business or to make distributions of monies received. It is an excellent vehicle for holding family assets whereby the children do, or eventually will, hold a majority interest but the parents still want to control the assets.

In Mary and Gary's case, they want to start gifting interests to their children in order to reduce their estate tax obligations. But they also want to control the assets in order to avoid them being squandered while their children aren't yet old enough to know money does not grow on trees.

There is one issue involving a Limited Partnership with which they have to deal: The general partner is personally liable for the debts of the LP. This is easily overcome by creating a Corporation or LLC to serve as the corporate general partner thus encapsulating the risk in a limited liability entity.

There are other advantages to the Limited Partnership that Mary and Gary like, including restrictions on transfers and limited liability. Mary and Gary decide to form M & G Holdings, LP to hold and protect their assets. As with John and Liz, we will come back to Mary and Gary's holding entity to see how they benefit from holding assets in a Limited Partnership.

Comparison of Entities

Sole Proprietorship

The easiest means of getting into business is to become a Sole Proprietor. You obtain a business license and a sales tax permit, comply with regulations that any other business has to follow and you are in business.

However, easier is not always better. The major drawback of a Sole Proprietorship is that its sole owner is completely liable for all business debts and claims. If someone falls on your property and your insurance does not cover it, your personal assets are at risk for the satisfaction of judgment. If you have a rough month and cannot pay the bills or the credit line to the bank, your personal bank account, and the equity in your house, your car and other personal assets can be attached for the repayment of judgments and debts.

In lectures given to aspiring entrepreneurs, I am always asked the question: "If I'm just starting out, why not be a Sole Proprietorship?" The answer is that you are never just starting out. You have accumulated assets throughout your life, and by using a Sole Proprietorship you are putting them at risk. The cost to form and maintain an LLC or Corporation is minimal compared to the risks involved in operating any form of business.

There are two statistics that support this position:

1. There are over 500,000 lawyers in America today.
2. One-third of all Americans will be sued at least once during their lifetime.

If you have ever been sued, you well know that it can be an extremely stressful and costly proposition. As an attorney I find many of my colleagues are honorable, but the sad truth is that the elements of justice, civility and fair play are often lost when some lawyers are involved. In addition, as many of you know, there are economic incentives in the system for lawyers to bring frivolous lawsuits. Until the courts start punishing improper lawyering, the only way to protect yourself is to remove all the assets you can from risk. Using a Sole Proprietorship or a General Partnership is not the way to do this.

If you have never been sued, please attempt to keep it that way. And as protection against it ever happening, take the legal and reasonable steps to put all of your personal assets out of the reach of potential business creditors.

The extra step needed to protect your personal assets from business risk is to submit filing documents with your secretary of state. Our affiliates provide this service for a very reasonable fee. There is even a 5 percent discount for the readers of this book found on page 278. Or, you can check into it yourself. By taking this step, and by following the minimal record keeping requirements associated with each entity, you can easily avoid the problems you may encounter with a Sole Proprietorship.

Another feature of the Sole Proprietorship to be considered is the fact that it may only have one owner. If your business grows and you bring in another owner, you are no longer a Sole Proprietorship. Once you start splitting the profits with another individual, your business becomes a General Partnership. And with that you are using an even less desirable entity for doing business than a Sole Proprietorship.

General Partnership

Whenever two or more persons agree to share profits and losses a partnership has been formed. Even if you never sign a Partnership Agreement, state law provides that under such circumstances you have formed a General Partnership.

A written Partnership Agreement is not required by law. A handshake is acceptable for formation. In the event you do not sign a formal document, you will be subject to your state's applicable partnership laws. This may not be to your advantage in that such general rules rarely satisfy specific situations. As an example, most states provide that profits and losses are to be divided equally among the partners. If your oral understanding is that you are to receive 75 percent of the profits, state law and your handshake will not help you. You are better advised to prepare a written agreement addressing your rights and rewards.

Unlike a Sole Proprietorship, in which only one individual may participate, by definition, a General Partnership must consist of two or more people. You cannot have a one-person partnership. On the other hand, you may have as many partners as you want in a General Partnership. This may sound like a blessing, but it is actually a curse.

The greatest drawback of a General Partnership is that each partner is liable for the debts and obligations incurred by all the other general partners. While you may trust the one general partner you have not to improperly obligate the partnership, the more general partners you bring aboard the greater risk you run that someone will mess up.

And remember, just as with Sole Proprietorships, your personal assets are at risk in a General Partnership. Your house and your life savings can be lost through the actions of your partner. While you may have had nothing to do with the decision that was made and you may have been five thousand miles away when it was made and you may have voiced your opposition to it when you found out it was made, as a general partner you are still personally responsible for that decision.

As such, a General Partnership is much riskier than a Sole Proprietorship. In a Sole Proprietorship, only the proprietor can bind the business. In a General Partnership, any general partner – no matter how wise or, unfortunately, how ignorant – may obligate the business. By contrast, LLCs and LPs and Corporations offer much greater protection. All of them offer owners limited personal liability for business debts and the acts of others.

It should be noted that because of these unlimited risks, the last thing you want to do is become a general partner of an enterprise in which you do not have day-to-day management control. If you do not thoroughly know what is going on in the company you should not put your future on the line as a general partner.

This issue occasionally arises when investment scam artists are trying to raise money through the sale of General Partnership interests. Because the sales of securities are so heavily regulated, and therefore costly to promote, certain unscrupulous types have promoted General Partnerships as an exception to the securities laws. Their slick rationale is that a General Partnership interest is not defined as a security since all general partners are manager/participants and thus not the type of passive investors for which the securities laws apply. Federal and state securities regulators do not agree with this definition. The interest you purchase allows you and several hundred other people to become general partners in, for example, "the most significant silver mining property in Bolivian history." The promoters raise the money and obligate the partnership to purchase several million dollars worth of mining equipment. Of course, the promoters then retire to Bolivia, leaving the remaining general partners liable for the partnership's debts. If you learn only one thing from this book it should be that you should absolutely never invest in a business as a passive general partner.

Certain advisors will, as with Sole Proprietorships, suggest that a General Partnership be used because it is easy to set up. Most states do not require organizational paperwork for a General Partnership to be filed with the secretary of state. Some advisors will comment that there is no requirement for a General Partnership to hold regular meetings or keep records of meetings, despite the fact that the better practice is to do so, and thus argue that General Partnerships are, again, easy.

As discussed with Sole Proprietorships, when it comes to General Partnerships, easier is not better. The specter of unlimited personal liability in this day and age is too overwhelming even for the lowliest aspiring start-up to take on. Furthermore, nothing about operating a business successfully is easy. Why then should one of the most important legal decisions you make about your business be "easy"?

There are two further arguments that certain advisors will make as to the easiness of General Partnerships. Both are fallacious and wrong.

In discussing the issue of unlimited personal liability for the acts of general partners, some will suggest that insurance can overcome such risks. This ignores the fact that many affordable commercial insurance policies contain:

- high deductibles for which the partners are responsible; and
- innumerable exclusions designed to limit coverage

Furthermore, most people involved in small businesses cannot foresee all the possible risks, and even if they could, would not be able to afford full coverage. No policy will cover the mismanagement of the partnership, much less the wrongful acts of one general partner. And no insurance is going to cover the inability of the partnership to pay its normal debts and obligations. Again, such acts become the personal responsibility of the general partners. On the other hand, LLCs and Corporations, as a matter of law, shield their owners from such liability.

A second argument made as to the easiness of the General Partnership is that all it takes is a simple General Partnership Agreement. As discussed, the need for a written document to reflect the partners' intent is prudent. However, the problem arises in that no General Partnership Agreement is simple. Each one must be tailored to reflect the specifics of the understanding and the transaction. The cost to have an attorney draft a General Partnership Agreement will run between $1,000 and $5,000. And with that, you are paying a significant amount of money for a document and an entity that will not protect you.

In my practice, I will not prepare a General Partnership Agreement for a client. It is simply not the right entity for any of my clients. Our associate, Altacian Corporate Services, prepares a complete and fully ready LLC, LP or Corporation for $695 in most cases, plus state filing fees. In doing so, we can better protect our clients and save them money in the process. Why should our clients pay more money to be put at greater risk?

I trust this initial discussion of Sole Proprietorships and General Partnership has dissuaded you from considering the use of such entities. They will be noted in the entity chart and in the section on taxation for purposes of comparison, but not seriously discussed hereafter.

Corporations

Forming a Corporation involves creating an independent legal entity with a life of its own. It has its own name, business purpose and tax identity with the IRS. As such, it – the Corporation – is responsible for the activities of the business. In this way, the owners, or shareholders, are protected. The owners' liability is limited to the monies they used to start the Corporation, not all of their other personal assets. If an entity is to be sued it is the Corporation, not the individuals behind this legal entity.

The history of Corporations can be traced to western civilization's rise from the stagnation of the Dark Ages. In the early 1500s it became apparent that a new form of business was needed in order to advance economic activity. Previously, an investor/entrepreneur who engaged in a business that was not successful would not only lose all of his personal assets. He also could be thrown into debtor's prison or hanged for his failings. How's that for encouraging risk? It wasn't really until the nation states of Europe needed their entrepreneurs to start competing for overseas opportunities that the limited liability corporate form of doing business was authorized and blossomed. And the result was one of the major catalysts for economic advancement out of the Dark Ages. When people are willing to take risks, and their personal assets can be protected in the process, societies will benefit.

A Corporation is organized by one or more shareholders. Depending upon each state's laws, it may allow one person to serve as all officers and directors. In certain states, to protect the owner's privacy, nominee officers and directors may be utilized. A Corporation's first filing, the Articles of

Incorporation, are signed by the incorporator. The incorporator may be any individual involved in the company, including frequently, the company's attorney.

The Articles of Incorporation set out the company's name, the initial Board of Directors, the authorized shares and other major items. Because it is a matter of public record, specific detailed or confidential information about the Corporation should not be included in the Articles of Incorporation. The Corporation is governed by rules found in its bylaws. Its decisions are recorded in meeting minutes, which are kept in the corporate minute book or corporate file.

When the Corporation is formed, the shareholders take over the company from the incorporator. The shareholders elect the directors to oversee the company. The directors in turn appoint the officers to carry out day-to-day management.

The shareholders, directors and officers of the company must remember to follow corporate formalities. They must treat the Corporation as a separate and independent legal entity, which includes holding regularly scheduled meetings, conducting banking through a separate corporate bank account, filing a separate corporate tax return and filing corporate papers with the state on a timely basis.

Failure to follow such formalities may allow a creditor to pierce the corporate veil and seek personal liability against the officers, directors and shareholders. Adhering to corporate formalities is not at all difficult or particularly time consuming. In fact, if you have your attorney handle the corporate filings and preparation of annual minutes and direct your accountant to prepare the corporate tax return, you should expend no extra time with only a very slight increase in cost. The point is that if you spend the extra money to form a Corporation in order to gain limited liability it makes sense to spend the extra, and minimal, time and money to insure that protection.

For some, a disadvantage of utilizing a regular Corporation (or C Corporation) to do business is that its earning may be taxed twice. This generally happens at the end of the

Corporation's fiscal year. As illustrated in the chart on page 17, if the Corporation earns a profit it pays a tax on the gain. If it then decides to pay a dividend from any after tax profits to its shareholders, the shareholders are taxed once again. However, through proper planning, the specter of double taxation can be minimized.

Nevertheless, this double taxation does not occur with a Limited Liability Company or a Limited Partnership. The flow-through taxation of Limited Liability Companies and Limited Partnerships represents, for many, a significant advantage over the corporate entity.

It should be noted here that a Corporation with flow-through taxation features does exist. The Sub-Chapter S Corporation (named after an IRS code section allowing it) is a flow-through corporate entity. By filing Form 2553, Election by a Small Business Corporation, the Corporation is not treated as a distinct entity for tax purposes. As a result, profits and losses flow through to the shareholders as in a partnership.

While a Sub-Chapter S Corporation is the entity of choice for certain small businesses, it does have some limits, as we discussed earlier. These limitations include the number of persons who could be shareholders, a prohibition against non United States residents from being shareholders, and prohibitions against other corporate entities, such as C Corporations, Limited Partnerships, Limited Liability Companies and other entities, including certain trusts, from being shareholders. Finally, a Sub-Chapter S Corporation may have only one class of stock.

In fact, it was the above-named limitations that, in part, lead to the adoption of the Limited Liability Company throughout the United States in the early 1990s. Because many shareholders wanted the protection of a Corporation with flow-through taxation but could not live within the shareholder limitations of a Sub-Chapter S Corporation, the Limited Liability Company was legislatively authorized.

The Sub-Chapter S Corporation requires the filing of IRS Form 2553 by the 15th day of the third month of its tax year for the flow-through tax election to become effective. A Limited Liability Company or Limited Partnership receives this treatment without the necessity of such a filing.

Another issue with a Sub-Chapter S Corporation is that flow-through taxation can be lost when one shareholder sells his stock to a non-permitted owner, such as a foreign individual or trust. By so terminating the Sub-Chapter S election, the business is then taxed as a C Corporation and the company cannot reelect S status for a period of five years. The potential for this problem is eliminated by using a Limited Liability Company.

Both C and S Corporations require that stock be issued to its shareholders. While Limited Liability Companies may issue membership interests and Limited Partnerships may issue partnership interests, they do not feature the same ease of transferability and liquidity of corporate shares. Neither Limited Liability Companies nor Limited Partnerships have the ability to offer an ownership incentive akin to stock options. Neither should either entity be considered a viable candidate for a public offering. If stock incentives and public tradability of shares is your objective, your first and only choice is to organize as a Corporation.

For a more complete discussion of corporate benefits and strategies, see my book, *Own Your Own Corporation* (Warner Books).

Limited Partnership

A Limited Partnership is similar to a General Partnership with the exception that it has two types of partners. The first type is a general partner who is responsible for managing the partnership. As with a General Partnership, the general partner of a Limited Partnership has broad powers to obligate the partnership and is also personally liable for the business's debts and claims. If there is more than one general partner involved they are all jointly and severally liable, meaning that a creditor can go after just one partner for the entire debt. (But as discussed below under Limited Liability, general partners can be protected in a Limited Partnership.) The second type of partner in a Limited Partnership is a limited partner. By definition, a limited partner is limited to his or her contribution of capital to the partnership and may not become actively involved in the business of the partnership. In the event a limited partner does become active in management, he or she may become personally responsible as a general partner.

To understand the management structure of a Limited Partnership, as well as an LLC and a Corporation, the following chart may be useful:

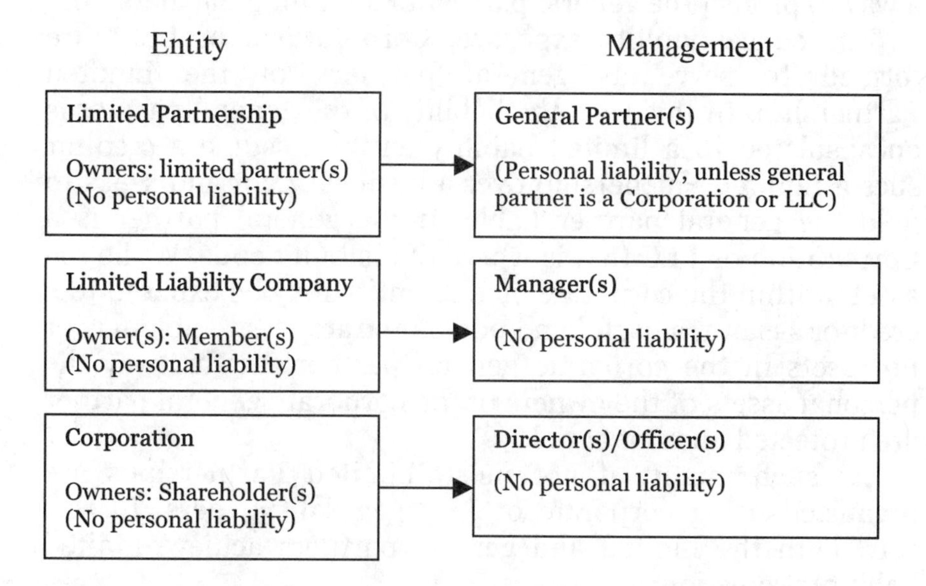

To organize a Limited Partnership you must file a Certificate of Limited Partnership, otherwise known as an LP-1, with the Secretary of State's office. This document contains certain information about the general partner and, depending on the state, limited partners, and is akin to the filing of

Articles of Incorporation for a Corporation or Articles of Organization for an LLC.

The Limited Partnership offers certain unique advantages not always found in other entities. These features include:

Limited Liability

Limited partners (limiteds) are not responsible for the partnership debts beyond the amount of their capital contribution or contribution obligation. So, as discussed, unless they become actively involved, the limiteds are protected.

As a rule, general partners are personally liable for all partnership debts. However, as was alluded to above, there is a way to protect the general partner of a Limited Partnership.

To reduce liability exposure, Corporations or LLCs are formed to serve as general partners of the Limited Partnership. In this way, the liability of the general partner is encapsulated in a limited liability entity. Assume a creditor sues a Limited Partnership over a business debt and seeks to hold the general partner liable. If the general partner is a Corporation or LLC that is where the liability ends. While the assets within the corporate or LLC entity may be exposed to a creditor's claim, a useful and popular strategy is to hold few or no assets in the corporate general partner. In this way the personal assets of the owners of the corporate general partner are protected and not at risk.

As such, many, if not most, Limited Partnerships are organized using corporate or LLC general partners. In this way, both the limited and general partners achieve limited liability protection.

Retained Management

By definition, limiteds may not participate in management, therefore the general partner maintains complete control. In many cases, the general partner will hold only two percent of the partnership interest but will be able to assert 100 percent control over the partnership. This feature is valuable in estate planning situations where a parent is gifting or has gifted Limited Partnership interests to his children.

Restrictions on Transfer

The ability to restrict the transfer of Limited or General Partnership interests to outside persons is a valuable feature of the Limited Partnership. Through a written Limited Partnership Agreement, rights of first refusal, prohibited transfers and conditions to permitted transfers are instituted to restrict the free transferability of partnership interests. It should be noted that LLCs can also afford beneficial restrictions on transfer. These restrictions are crucial for achieving the creditor protection and estate and gift tax advantages afforded by Limited Partnerships.

Protection from Creditors

Creditors of a partnership can only reach the partnership assets and the assets of the general partner, which is limited by using a corporate general partner. Thus if, for example, you and your family owned three separate apartment buildings, it may be prudent to compartmentalize these assets into three separate Limited Partnerships, using three separate corporate general partners. If a litigious tenant sued over conditions at one of the properties, the other two buildings would not be exposed to satisfy any claims.

Creditors of the individual partners can only reach that person's partnership interest and not the partnership assets themselves. Assume you've gifted a Limited Partnership interest equal to 25 percent in one of the apartment building partnerships to your son. He is young and forgets to obtain automobile insurance. Of course, in this example he gets in a car accident and has a judgment creditor looking for assets. This creditor cannot reach the apartment building asset itself because it is in the Limited Partnership. He can only reach the money earned by your son's 25 percent Limited Partnership interest, and then only, in many states, through the charging order procedure. Charging orders, which can result in phantom income to the creditor, are discussed more fully in Chapter Seven, and are not favored by creditors.

Family Wealth Transfers

With proper planning, transfers of family assets from one generation to the next can occur at discounted rates. As a general rule, the IRS, at the time of this writing, allows one individual to give another individual a gift of $11,000 per year. Any gifts valued at over $11,000 are subject to a gift tax, again, at the time of this writing, starting at 18 percent. In the estate-planning arena, senior family members may be advised to give assets away during their lifetimes so that estate taxes of up to 55 percent are minimized. And please note, while Congress has claimed to have gradually eliminated estate taxes over a ten year period, the law, as it is currently written, brings estate taxes right back up to their previously high levels, starting in 2011. The legislation, as enacted in the Spring of 2001, is one of the worst examples of Congressional duplicity ever recorded. Do not count on the "promise" of estate tax elimination. Congress can and will reinstate such taxes whenever they can. To be prudent, you must continue your estate planning and family gifting strategies.

By using a Family Limited Partnership – a Limited Partnership formed and utilized for the management and gifting of family assets – gifting can be accelerated with an IRS-approved discount. Because Limited Partnership interests do not entitle the holder to take part in management affairs and are frequently restricted as to their transferability, discounts on their value are permissible. In other words, even if the book value of 10 percent of a certain Limited Partnership is $14,000, a normal investor wouldn't pay that much for it because, as a limited, he or she would have no say in the partnership's management and would be restricted in his or her ability to transfer interest at a later date. So, instead of valuing that Limited Partnership interest at $14,000, the IRS recognizes that it may be worth more like $11,000.

The advantage of this recognition comes into play when parents are ready to gift to their children. Assume a husband and wife have four children. Each spouse can gift $11,000 per year to each child without paying a gift tax. As such, a total of $88,000 can be gifted each year (two parents x four children x $11,000 per child). With the valuation discount reflecting that the $14,000 interest is only worth $11,000 to a normal investor, each parent gifts a 10 percent Limited Partnership interest to each child. Their combined gifts are valued at $88,000, thus incurring no gift tax. However, the parents have gifted away 80 percent of the Limited Partnership. The 80 percent interest has a book value of $112,000. Had the parents not used a Limited Partnership they would have had to pay a gift tax on the $24,000 difference between the $112,000 book value and the $88,000 discounted value.

Estate planning will be discussed in greater depth in Chapter Eight.

Flexibility

The Limited Partnership provides a great deal of flexibility. A written Limited Partnership Agreement can be drafted to tailor the business and family planning requirements of any situation. And there are very few statutory requirements that cannot be changed or eliminated through a well-drafted Partnership Agreement.

Taxation

Limited Partnerships, like General Partnerships, are flow-through tax entities. The Limited Partnership files an informational partnership tax return (IRS Form 1065, United States Partnership Return of Income, the same as a General

Partnership) and each limited receives an IRS Schedule K-1 (1065), Partner's Share of Income, Credits and Deductions, from the Limited Partnership. Each limited then files the K-1 with his or her individual IRS 1040 tax return. The issue of taxation will be discussed more fully in Chapter Four.

Limited Liability Company

A Limited Liability Company is a new form of entity introduced into the United States in 1977. The LLC combines certain advantages of partnerships and Corporations and has been called an "incorporated partnership."

Genesis of the LLC

The Limited Liability Company can be traced to a German entity known as the Gesellschaft mit beschranker Haftung (GmbH). Created in 1892 and combining limited liability with flow-through taxation, this entity soon found converts in a number of Latin American and European countries, including Portugal (1901); Panama (1917); Brazil (1919); France (1925); Chile (1929); Argentina (1932); Uruguay (1933); Mexico (1934); Belgium (1935); Switzerland (1936); Italy (1936); Peru (1936); Columbia (1937); Costa Rica (1942) and Honduras (1950).

As United States businesses engaged in international commerce after World War II, many became exposed to the benefits of these foreign LLCs. Finally, Hamilton Brothers, an oil exploration firm that had used LLCs throughout Latin America, saw the benefits of the United States offering such an entity. They lobbied the Wyoming legislature to enact LLC legislation and effective June 30, 1977, Wyoming became the first state to offer LLCs. Florida followed in 1982, and by 1994 all 50 states had enacted permitting legislation.

One of the primary advantages of an LLC is that no one has personal liability, as in a Limited Partnership. As discussed, the general partner of a Limited Partnership is personally liable for the debts of the partnership. The way to minimize this is to form a separate Corporation or LLC to serve as the general partner, thus encapsulating personal liability within a protected entity.

However, with an LLC, both managers and members (akin to the directors and officers and shareholders of a Corporation) are free from personal liability. This LLC feature removes the need to form a separate Corporation or LLC manager.

LLCs also offer the previously mentioned Limited Partnership features of restrictions on transfers and protection from creditors. LLCs are also useful for family wealth transfers, although some CPAs and estate planning professionals are more comfortable using Limited Partnerships for this purpose.

Flow-Through Taxation

As has been mentioned throughout, one of the most significant benefits of the LLC, and a key reason for its existence, is the fact that the IRS recognizes it as a pass-through tax entity. All of the profits and losses of the business flow through the LLC without tax. They flow through to the business, real estate, or asset-holding owner's tax return and are dealt with at the individual level.

Again, a C Corporation does not offer such a feature. In a C Corporation, the profits are taxed at the corporate level and then taxed again when a dividend is paid to the shareholder – thus the issue of double taxation. In a Sub S Corporation, profits and losses flow through the Corporation, thereby avoiding double taxation, but may only be allocated to the shareholders according to their percentage ownership interest. As described below, LLC profits and losses flow through the entity and may be allocated in a flexible manner without regard to ownership percentages. As such, the LLC offers the combination of two significant financial benefits that other entities do not.

Flexible Ownership

In 1997, the IRS abandoned its creaky rules on tax classification, allowing for single-member LLCs. State legislatures immediately followed suit and amended their statutes to allow for single-member LLCs. To date, only Massachusetts still requires two members to form an LLC.

As a result, you can now form an LLC and be the sole member. You can enjoy the benefits of limited liability and flow-through taxation and not answer to anyone (except, of course, possibly your spouse and the IRS). And, because the IRS views a single-member LLC as a "disregarded entity" for tax purposes, you may not even need to file an LLC tax return. Instead, the LLC's profits and losses can flow directly onto Schedule C, E, or F (depending on the type of trade or business carried on by your single-member LLC) of your personal IRS return. And, a single-member can also include a husband and wife as joint tenants, or a living trust. Better yet, while the IRS views a single-member LLC as a disregarded entity (thus obviating the need for an LLC tax return), the law still views a single-member LLC as being entitled to limited liability protection.

But for every benefit comes a drawback. There are two cases, one in California and one in Colorado, where the court has found that a single-member LLC is not entitled to asset protection benefits. Whether this judicial view will expand to other states remains to be seen. But, when weighing the advantage of no LLC tax return, you've got to weigh it against a possible loss of entity protection. Many people may choose to have a two or more member LLC just to be safe, and to file an LLC tax return as necessary.

Another flexibility benefit has to do with ownership. One of the reasons that people have a problem utilizing the Sub S

Corporation is the limit on owners. When LLCs were created, a Sub S Corporation could only have 35 or fewer shareholders. The IRS has since raised that number to 75. Certain foreign citizens and domestic entities are still prohibited from becoming shareholders of a Sub S Corporation.

The LLC offers the flexibility of allowing from one member to an unlimited number of members, each of whom may be a foreign citizen, trust or a corporate entity. And unlike a Sub-Chapter S Corporation, you won't have to worry about losing your flow-through taxation in the event one shareholder sells his or her shares to a prohibited shareholder.

Flexible Management

LLCs offer two very flexible and workable means of management. First, they can be managed by all of their members, which is known as member-managed. Or they can be managed by just one or some of the members or by an outside nonmember, which is called manager-managed.

It is very easy to designate whether the LLC is to member- or manager-managed. In some states, the Articles of Organization filed with the state must set out how the LLC is to be managed. In other jurisdictions, management is detailed in the Operating Agreement. If the members of an LLC want to change from manager-managed to member-managed, or vice versa, such a change can be accomplished by a vote of the members.

In most cases, the LLC will be managed by the members. In a small, growing company, each owner will want to have an active say in how the business is operated. Member management is a direct and simple way to accomplish this.

It should be noted that in a Corporation there are several layers of management supervision. The officers – president, secretary, treasurer and vice presidents – handle the day-to-day affairs. They are appointed by the board of directors, which oversees the larger, strategic issues of the Corporation. The directors are elected by the shareholders. By contrast, in a member-managed LLC the members are the shareholders, directors and officers all at once.

In some cases, such as the following, manager management is appropriate for conducting the business of the LLC:

1. One or several LLC members are only interested in investing in the business and want no part of management decision-making.
2. A family member has gifted membership interests to his or her children but does not want them (perhaps because they are not ready) to take part in management decisions.
3. A nonmember has lent money to the LLC and wants a say in how the funds are spent. The solution is to adopt manager management and make him a manager.
4. A group of members come together and invest in a business. They feel it is prudent to hire a professional outside manager to run the business and give him or her management authority.

As with a Corporation, it is advisable to keep minutes of the meetings held by those making management decisions. While some states do not require annual or other meetings of an LLC, the better practice is to document such meetings on a consistent basis in order to avoid miscommunication, claims for mismanagement or attempts to assert personal liability.

Distribution of LLC Profits and Losses

One of the remarkable features of an LLC is that members may divide the profits and losses in a flexible manner. This is a significant departure from the corporate regime whereby dividends and distributions, respectively, are allocated according to percentage ownership.

As an example, Red, Blue and Tiny each own one third of a business. Red puts in all of the money, Blue does all the work and Tiny doesn't do much of anything. The business loses $90,000 the first year and makes $120,000 the second year.

In a Sub-Chapter S Corporation, the three would each be allocated a loss of $30,000 the first year and a gain of $40,000 in the second year. Red and Blue are understandably not too keen on this distribution scheme.

In contrast with an LLC, Red could be allocated all of the losses in the first year and Blue could be allocated a large percentage of the gain in the second year. As long as certain special tax split rules are met and each individual pays the taxes on the gains he or she receives, the IRS is amenable to this flexible approach. And in the reality of the business world, where some people put up the money, some do most of the work and a few do absolutely nothing at all, the flexibility of LLC distributions can make all the difference between moving forward and getting bogged down in squabbling over who is doing what.

Lack of Precedent

One of the drawbacks to the LLC is the fact that it is a new entity. As such, there are not many court decisions defining the various aspects of its use. With Corporations and partnerships, on the other hand, you have several hundred years of court cases creating a precedent for operation.

Most legal commentators anticipate that the courts will look to corporate law to define the limited liability and corporate features of the LLC and to partnership law to define the partnership aspects of the entity. In time, a cohesive body of LLC law will emerge.

Until that day arrives, owners of an LLC must be cognizant that the courts may interpret a feature, a benefit or even a wrinkle of LLC law in a way that does not suit them. If you are on the fence between selecting a Limited Partnership, a Corporation or an LLC and do not like the uncertainty associated with a lack of legal precedent, you may want to consider utilizing an entity other than an LLC.

The greatest concern I have with the absence of LLC legal precedence deals with how the courts will "pierce the LLC veil" and impose personal liability upon the members. I assume that the courts will track the reasons and means for piercing the veil in line with a corporate situation. We shall discuss this issue in greater detail throughout the book.

In a corporate scenario one can easily avoid the imposition of personal liability by simply following certain corporate formalities. These include:

1. Timely filings with the state.
2. Preparation of corporate tax returns.
3. Maintaining a separate bank account.
4. Separating personal and business matters.
5. Adequate capitalization of the company.
6. Annual meetings of directors and shareholders.

In the LLC scenario, the first five requirements apply anyway in order to maintain your status. As with a Corporation, you will need to prepare a tax return for each member to reflect the business results of the LLC (unless, as discussed, you are a single-member LLC). In addition, while not all states require annual meetings of the members, as mentioned above, the better practice is to hold such meetings. When some court some day holds that, despite no state requirement to do so, failure to hold member meetings is evidence of a lack of LLC formality you will want to have a minute book chock full of annual meeting minutes to overcome any such challenge.

By adhering to the formalities a Corporation is required to follow to avoid piercing the corporate veil, it is anticipated that members of an LLC will avoid having their LLC veil pierced in the future.

The chart on the following pages illustrates some of the differences and similarities between the various entities we have discussed.

	Limited Liability Company	Limited Partnership	General Partnership	S Corporation	C Corporation	Sole Proprietorship
Personal liability for business debts	No personal liability of members	General Partner(s) personally liable; limited partners no personally liable	General Partner(s) personally liable	No personal liability of shareholder(s)	No personal liability of shareholder(s)	Sole Proprietor personally liable
Who can legally obligate the business?	A member where member-managed; a manager where manager-managed	Any General Partner (but not by limiteds)	Any General Partner	Officers and Directors	Officers and Directors	Sole Proprietor
Responsibility for management decisions	Same as above	Same as above	General Partners	Officers and Directors	Officers and Directors	Sole Proprietor
Ownership Restrictions	Most states allow single-member LLCs	One General Partner and one limited required	At least two General Partners	No more than 75 shareholders; no foreign entities or individuals or domestic entities	Most states allow one shareholder corporations, some states require two or more shareholders	Only one Sole Proprietor
Start-up and ongoing formalities	Articles filed with state; Operating Agreement and Annual Meetings not required but strongly recommended	LP-1 filed with state; Partnership Agreement and Annual Meetings not required but strongly recommended	No state filing; Partnership Agreement recommended, no Annual Meeting required	Articles filed with state; Form 2553 filed with IRS; Bylaws and Annual Meetings required	Articles filed with state; Bylaws and Annual Meetings required	No state filing; to Annual Meeting required
Limits on transferability of interests	Unanimous or supermajority consent may be required by non-transferring member(s)	Consent of all limiteds (if applicable) may be required	Consent of all partners may be required	Transfers may be limited by agreement or by securities laws; transfers to non-qualified persons may cause loss of S Corporation status	Transfers may be limited by agreement or by securities laws	Can sell business to another

	Limited Liability Company	Limited Partnership	General Partnership	S Corporation	C Corporation	Sole Proprietorship
Business effect on death or departure of owner	In some states dissolution, unless member(s) vote to continue the LLC	Automatic dissolution unless provided for in Limited Partnership Agreement	Automatic dissolution unless provided for in Partnership Agreement	Corporation continues	Corporation continues	Automatic dissolution
Taxation of business profits	Individual tax rates of member(s) unless LLC elects corporate taxation (California LLCs pay additional state fees)	Individual tax rates of general and limiteds (Texas taxation laws favor use of LPs)	Individual tax rates of general partners	Corporate profits taxed at individual shareholder(s) rates	Tax paid at corporate level, then tax is paid on distributions by shareholders	Individual tax rate of Sole Proprietor

With our overview and comparison completed, it is now time to consider the various specific issues associated with using and operating Limited Liability Companies and Limited Partnerships. But first, here are some commonly asked questions and their answers regarding LLCs and LPs.

Frequently Asked Questions

When should I use an LLC over an LP and vice-versa?

Since everyone's situation is different there is no definitive and correct answer to this question. As a general rule, some planners will more frequently use LPs for estate planning and holding purposes and LLCs for operating businesses. However, there can be valid reasons to use LLCs and LPs for holding and operating businesses, respectively. If you have a question in your own mind, you and your professional advisor should arrive at the entity best suited for you specific needs.

Is there a difference in liability protection between an LLC and an LP?

The one major difference is that in an LP the general partner is personally liable for the debts and obligations of the Limited Partnership, and the limited partners, by acting as generals, may become personally liable as well. In an LLC, managers and members are not personally exposed. Please note that in an LLC, LP or even a Corporation, individuals may be held personally responsible for fraudulent and willful misconduct as well as for the failure to pay payroll taxes to the IRS. Limited liability protection does not extend to intentional bad acts.

Can non-United States citizens be members of an LLC or partners in an LP?

Yes. While non-resident aliens (foreign individuals living outside the United States) may not be shareholders of Sub-

Chapter S Corporations, they may own interests in and be involved in management of an LLC, LP or C Corporation.

Can an LLC or LP own stock in a Sub-Chapter S Corporation?

No. Neither can a C corporation, irrevocable trust or a non-resident alien.

If I use a C Corporation as the manager of an LLC or the general partner of an LP, should I open a bank account in the name of the C Corporation or the LLC/LP?

You may need to open two bank accounts. The business or holding entity will need a bank account for its purposes. The C Corporation, if it receives a management fee from the LLC/LP, will need a bank account to receive and disburse the income it receives.

What is a "Partnership in Commendam?"

In Louisiana, a Limited Partnership is known as a "partnership in commendam."

How many pieces of income-producing property should be held in one LP or LLC?

Again, there is no correct answer here. The overall strategy is to segregate assets. You don't want a judgment creditor (one with a court-approved claim against you) to be able to reach ten properties in one entity. But does that mean that each entity holds one asset or four assets? That is a judgment call for you to decide. I have some clients who are not troubled by the annual fees and put only one asset into one entity in order to completely segregate assets. I have others who feel that three assets per entity is the right number. You must arrive at your own decision.

How many general partners and limited partners may an LP have?

There are no limits. Of course, you must follow the securities laws when bringing in large numbers of investors.

How many managers and members may an LLC have?

Again, there are no limits subject to application of the securities laws.

Would you suggest an LLC or an LP to hold a large securities portfolio?

I would suggest one or the other depending upon your circumstances. For estate planning and control purposes some planners would more often use an LP. In a situation where several persons were owners and all wanted a say in management, a member-managed LLC may be appropriate.

Can my wife and I own 100 percent of a corporate general partner that owns 2 percent of an LP and also individually own the remaining 98 percent of the LP as limited partners?

Yes. This scenario is frequently used in Family Limited Partnerships and is not considered to be too closely held.

Can the same 2 percent general partner Corporation also own the 98 percent Limited Partnership interests?

No. In that case, there are not two partners as required for an LP.

Chapter Two
Entity Formation

<u>Case Numbers 1 & 2 – John and Liz; Mary and Gary</u>

John and Liz are ready to form J & L Consulting, LLC. Mary and Gary are likewise ready to form M & G Holdings, LP. How do they proceed?

Limited Liability Company

With an LLC, Articles of Organization are filed with the secretary of state's office of the state in which you wish to operate. Before the Articles are filed the organizers must determine if they are to be member-managed or manager-managed and who the managers will be. A resident agent (an individual or corporate entity that will agree to accept service of legal documents on your behalf) must be identified and accept the appointment. An Operating Agreement is then prepared which further details the rights and responsibilities of the managers and members and outlines the operating procedures for the entity.

Limited Partnership

With a Limited Partnership, a Certificate of Limited Partnership (LP-1) is filed with the secretary of state. Likewise, before the LP-1 is filed the partners must determine who is going to serve as the general partner and a resident agent must be identified.

A Limited Partnership Agreement is then drafted which, as in the LLC Operating Agreement, details important entity issues. It should be noted here that a discussion of how to draft Operating and Partnership Agreements far exceeds the scope of this book, and is indeed a book unto itself. For now, we shall discuss what points and strategies should be contained in these agreements so that you and your professional advisor can come up with the document that is right for you.

Which State to Use?

A common formation issue for LLCs and LPs is which state to utilize for filing. To answer this question the following must be considered:

1. In what state – or states – will the company operate?
2. Is the company willing to pay extra to file in a more favorable state?

Case Number 1 – John and Liz

John and Liz know that J & L Consulting, LLC will operate in a number of states right away. They already have clients lined up in California, Nevada, Texas and Florida. They have been advised by their accountant that by going into Florida, for example, they will need to have their company qualified to do business in Florida. This entails filing as a foreign (or out of state) LLC with the Florida secretary of state's office.

The decision then for John and Liz is which state to use for the original formation. With their professional advisor they review the LLC statutes for the four states in question. They decide on Nevada because it offers the advantage of greater protections for managers. After filing originally in Nevada they then go ahead and qualify as a foreign LLC doing business in California, Texas and Florida (already being aware of the special state tax issues associated with California LLCs, as addressed in one of the last questions in Chapter Four). They realize that they will have to pay annual fees in each state as well as, where applicable, file an annual tax return to each state. However, John and Liz know that these are the costs of doing business and they sleep better at night knowing they are following the rules. In addition, they know that if they have not registered they could be prohibited from bringing a lawsuit or transacting any future business in the state(s) in question.

Case Number 2 – Mary and Gary

Mary and Gary live in California and the first asset they seek to protect is a four-plex apartment building they are purchasing in California. Mary and Gary have learned that LPs (and LLCs) are effective asset protection entities, in part because of the charging order procedure (See Chapter Seven for details on what a charging order is and how it works). However, they have also learned that California law (and so far only California law) is such that in some cases the charging order procedure is not the best remedy. In two cases (discussed on page 152), California courts have ignored the charging order procedure and allowed partnership interests to be reached by a creditor.

This disturbs Mary and Gary. They want to protect their assets, not expose them. After reviewing the situation with their professional advisors they decide to use a Nevada LP to hold the apartment building – and then qualify that entity to do business in California.

Of course, this means that they have to spend more money than is ordinarily required. If California law had been favorable they could have originally filed in California and be done. But they want to assert that Nevada law, which has never overturned or ignored the charging order remedy and has legislatively made it the exclusive remedy for creditors, will apply. (Later we will review the benefits of Nevada and Wyoming law.) While there is no guarantee that a California court hearing such a case will apply Nevada law, at least Mary and Gary, by creating a Nevada LP and qualifying it in California, can make the Nevada argument.

And so Mary and Gary find themselves in the position of paying extra to be in a more favorable state. For them it is worth another several hundred dollars per year to use a Nevada LP.

As they proceeded both Mary and Gary and John and Liz learn it is also important to consider the specific issues associated with each document, as outlined below:

Limited Liability Companies

As mentioned, the first step in organizing an LLC is to prepare and file the Articles of Organization. While each state has different rules, there are common requirements:

Articles of Organization

LLC Name: Check for name availability with your state's secretary of state. Consider separately trademarking and protecting the name within your state through your local secretary of state or within the country through the United States Trademark Office. (Visit www.sutlaw.com for more information on trademarking.)

Purposes and Powers: You must make a statement about what kind of business your entity will engage in. Many states allow a broad, unlimited purpose and power to be stated, essentially saying that your entity has all rights available to it in that state to engage in giving your entity full power to engage in any and all legal businesses within that state.

Name and Address of Resident Agent: To provide claimants with an office in the state upon which to serve lawsuits, a resident agent must be obtained and a registered address listed. Please note that, as with LPs and Corporations, if you live in your state of organization you can serve as your own resident agent, although you may not want to do so. Most corporate entities that act as resident agents charge a yearly fee for this service.[1]

---

[1] You may want to visit www.altacian.com for more information on resident agent services. They offer the service for $125 per year, but that price also includes annual benefits valued at over $500.

Manager-Managed or Member Managed: Unlike an LP or Corporation, either all of the members or a manager may run the LLC. Usually, this decision must be stated in the Articles of Organization.

Operating Agreement

Like the bylaws of a Corporation, the Operating Agreement provides the rules for operation of the LLC. Common provisions likely to be found are:

Managers: The number of managers, the term, election and removal of managers will all be set out.

Restrictions on Transfer of Interests: Unlike shares of a Corporation, the transfer of LLC membership interests is more complicated. The rules are set out in the Operating Agreement.

Distributions to Members: Profits and Losses: Profit distributions and loss allocations are governed by partnership law, which is different from the laws governing payment of dividends in a Corporation. The rules for partnership law are more complex and are set out in the Operating Agreement.

Meetings: Many states leave the whole need for meetings up to the members. We suggest that annual meetings be held to satisfy entity formality issues. Any requirements should be set out in the Operating Agreement.

Charging Order: Although many states require creditors to follow the charging order procedure as a matter of state law, it is a good idea to include it in the Operating Agreement.

Other Requirements: You should also be aware of any requirements that your own state's statute may have regarding Operating Agreements. For example, Nevada law (Nevada Revised Statutes (NRS) 86.286) provides:

> "A limited liability company may, but is not required to, adopt an operating agreement. An operating

agreement may be adopted only by the unanimous vote or unanimous written consent of the members, and the operating agreement must be in writing. Unless otherwise provided in the operating agreement, amendments to the agreement may be adopted only by the unanimous vote or unanimous written consent of the persons who are members at the time of amendment."

Limited Partnerships

To organize an LP, most states require that a certificate of Limited Partnership (LP-1) be filed with the secretary of state. As mentioned with LLCs, while each state may have unique requirements, the following are common requirements:

Certificate of Limited Partnership

Limited Partnership Name: As with the other entities, check on name availability with the secretary of state and remember that there are separate trademark requirements.

General Character of Business: "General character" is another way of saying "business purpose." You need not be too specific in most states (i.e., you can describe the general character of the partnership as "to conduct any legal form of business in that state").

Name and Address of Resident Agent: As discussed throughout the book, it is important to list a resident agent that will be in business next year.

Name and Address of General Partner: Some states also require the names and addresses of all limited partners.

Amounts of Contributions: Not all states require this and for good reason. Not many investors want it on the public record that they put $10 million into Wild Oats, LP. That kind of information is better kept within the company.

Duration: Many states limit a Limited Partnership to only 30 years duration. You must specify a termination date.

Events of Termination/Dissolution: Some states require the certificate of Limited Partnership to state what triggers dissolution or termination.

Limited Partnership Agreement

The Limited Partnership Agreement, like the LLC's Operating Agreement and a Corporation's bylaws, sets out the road map for operations. Common provisions include:

Management by General Partner: The agreement will set out the duties of the general partner. Unless limited by the Partnership Agreement, the general partner(s) will have broad authority to obligate and operate the partnership. It is important to consider these issues when drafting the agreement. You may want to limit the authority of the general partner(s).

Limited Partners' Role: The rights, powers and voting rights of the limiteds will be set out in the Partnership Agreement. Again, you may draft the agreement according to your own strategy and procedure, subject to the overall foundational requirement that limiteds do not get involved with management. Nevertheless, flexibility is allowed, as evidenced by Nevada's law that:

> "The partnership agreement may grant to all or certain identified general partners the right to vote on a per capita or any other basis, separately or with all or any class of the limited partners, on any matter." (NRS 88.465)
>
> ***
>
> "... the partnership agreement may grant to all or a specified group of the limited partners the right to vote on a per-capita or other basis upon any matter." (NRS 88.425)

Restrictions on Transfers/Distributions to Partners: As is true for LLCs, partnerships can be fairly complex with regard to these issues. Oftentimes partners are restricted from selling their interests to an outside third party. These issues should be dealt with in great detail in the Partnership Agreement.

Events of Termination/Dissolution: Because Limited Partnerships generally have a fixed duration (e.g. 30 or 99 years) the provisions for termination and dissolution should be detailed.

Charging Order: As with LLCs, you may want to provide that a charging order is a creditor's exclusive remedy. Again, this is the most effective way to keep LP assets out of the reach of would-be creditors.

Frequently Asked Questions

What are some of the issues to be considered when forming an LLC or an LP?

The following issues should be reviewed when forming any entity:

1. Business Continuity.
2. Formation Costs.
3. Time for Formation.
4. Federal Taxation.
5. State Taxation.
6. Tax Consequences of Formation.
7. Tax Consequences Upon Sale or Transfer.
8. Management and Control.
9. Liability of Owners.
10. Transferability of Interest.
11. Ability to Raise Capital.
12. Estate Planning Opportunities.

When does the LLC/LP come into existence?

In most states existence for an LP or LLC occurs upon filing of the certificate of Limited Partnership or Articles of Organization, respectively. Most states also provide that a certified copy of such documents from the secretary of state's office is conclusive evidence of formation.

What are the consequences of a rejected filing?

The secretary of state's office may reject a filing of articles or a certificate for a number of reasons. These include a failure to pay the filing fee, entity name already in use and failure to provide a resident agent. Generally, the state will send back the paperwork and identify the problem.

The consequence of this is that until those documents are properly prepared and filed the members or partners are personally liable for all business debts. As such, it is best to have your accepted and certified paperwork from the state in hand before you begin obligating the business, or yourself.

Is an LLC required to have an Operating Agreement or an LP to have a Partnership Agreement?

These agreements are not required in some states and may be oral in others. The better practice is to have a written agreement defining the operation of the entity.

Are all of the member/partner of an LLC/LP required to sign the Operating/Partnership Agreement?

Some states require that all members/partners adopt the agreement. However, in states where this is not required, those members/partners who do not sign the agreement may not be bound by its terms. It is far better practice to have each member/partner sign the agreement and consent to be bound by it.

How are Articles of Organization or Certificate of Limited Partnership amended?

Most states provide that these documents may be amended at any time. In some cases, such as a change of name or duration, they must be amended. The procedure involves an authorized person(s) filing a certificate of amendment with the secretary of state's office.

It is important to note that an amendment to a provision that originally required, for example, a 75 percent vote of the members or limiteds, must be approved and amended by at least a 75 percent vote of the members or limiteds. Please also note that some states require a unanimous vote to amend the filings.

How are an Operating Agreement and a Partnership Agreement amended?

Operating Agreements and Partnership Agreements are amended by a vote of the members or partners. Again, some states require a unanimous vote to amend these agreements.

Why would you amend an Operating Agreement or a Partnership Agreement?

There are a number of reasons to amend these agreements. For example, you may want to change the existing procedures for admission of new members/partners or removal of a manager or general partners. You may want to add a new procedure for the review of major acquisition decisions. The key is that if you want to change the agreement, a vote of the members/partners is needed.

What does a registered or resident agent do?

The purpose of a registered or resident agent (they are the same thing) is to accept service of process (lawsuits) in their state of residence. A registered agent, whose office is the registered office and which may be separate from the entity's business headquarters, is required so that claimants can easily locate and serve corporate, LLC, LP and other entities. If the resident agent or registered office changes the entity must file a notice of such change with the secretary of state's office.

Be sure to use resident agents that will be in business several years from now. Because they are authorized to receive notices of a lawsuit against your entity you want to be certain they appreciate the importance of this and provide you prompt notice. The last thing you want is to be sued and have a default judgment entered because you never received notice of the claim. Only use a reputable resident agent service. Expect to pay resident agent fees on a yearly basis, which can range from $100 to several hundred dollars per year, depending on the resident agent. Our affiliate, Altacian Corporate Services, offers yearly resident agent services for $125.00 per year.

Do LLCs/LPs have bylaws?

No, LLCs/LPs do not have bylaws. The Operating Agreement for the LLC and the Partnership Agreement for the LP serve as the bylaws for each entity.

When is an entity considered to be doing business in another state?

Unfortunately, most states do not define what constitutes doing business in their state. Instead, the question must be approached by reviewing what some states consider not doing business in their state. These include:

1. Maintaining bank accounts.
2. Selling goods through an independent contractor.
3. Soliciting or obtaining orders, whether by mail or employees or agents, if the orders require acceptance outside the state before a valid contract is formed.

4. Maintaining, defending or settling any lawsuit or other legal proceeding.
5. Holding meetings of members or managers or carrying on other activities concerning internal affairs.
6. Conducting an isolated transaction that is completed within a short period of time, such as 30 days, and is not a repeated transaction.

When an entity is doing business in another state, how is it registered?

Each state has its own guidelines. Generally, a filing fee and the following information is required:

1. Name of the foreign LLC or foreign LP (with foreign meaning out-of-state).
2. Date of formation.
3. Nature of business and purpose.
4. State of organization.
5. Statement that the foreign entity validly exists in the state of organization.
6. Address of the registered office and name of registered agent within the state.
7. Address of the office in the state of organization or the principal office.

In some cases certified copies of the LLC Articles or LP-1 along with a Certificate of Good Standing are required. Our affiliate, Altacian Corporate Services, assists companies to qualify in new states. It is not an overly complicated process, but one that must be done right and on a timely basis for protection to apply.

Can family members be partners in a Family Limited Partnership?

Yes, but only if one of the following requirements is met:

1. If capital (i.e. investment in machinery, equipment or inventory) is a material factor, a partner must have

acquired his or her ownership interest in a bona fide transaction (by gift or purchase) and must actually own or control such interest; or

2. If capital is not a material factor, the partners must have provided some contribution (services or capital) for their interest and come together in good faith to conduct a business.

How is an Operating Agreement or a Partnership Agreement enforceable?

Many states provide that such agreements may be enforced by that state's courts. Because these agreements are considered contracts by law, when a state's statute is silent on the issue, state law will apply to enforce binding legal contracts. Nevertheless, as is always the case, an oral agreement may be difficult to enforce.

Chapter Three
Entity Management

In every business, one or more people need to take care of day-to-day operations. In an LLC, management is by managers or members. In an LP, management is by the general partner. As the rules for each are slightly different, we shall consider each separately.

Limited Liability Company Management

There are two methods of management for an LLC – member management and manager management. Under most state statutes, all members of an LLC are equally responsible for its management. Where all members are actively involved in managing the business, as is frequently the case with many smaller businesses, the LLC is member-managed. On the other hand, the LLC may select to be managed by only some of its members or by a nonmember altogether. This is known as a manager-managed LLC.

It is a requirement in most states that you identify whether you are manager- or member-managed as part of your Articles of Organization filing with the state. (Please note that in Minnesota and North Dakota managers are referred to as "governors.") Although at least one manager (member or otherwise) is required, there is no upward limit on the number of managers you may have. To change from one form of management to the other will generally require the consent of the members (in some cases by a super majority, or greater than a majority, vote) and may also require the amendment of your Operating Agreement and possibly the filing with your state of an amendment to your Articles of Organization.

Member Management

As mentioned, in the typical two or more member active LLC scenario, several individuals have come together to make a go at a business. For each individual the business is his or her current provider and his or her future hope. As such, it is perfectly reasonable and understandable that each member wants to have a say in how the business is run.

Case Number 1 – John and Liz

J & L Consulting, LLC is operated by John and Liz. They are the only members and the only people involved in running the business, thus the only managers. In almost all cases, it would not be appropriate or fair to ask one of them to refrain from managing the LLC. It is also not really necessary to create a separate class of managers to be elected by the members. Accordingly, John and Liz decide to be member-managed, whereby each member is also a manager. In corporate terms this would be the same as agreeing that every shareholder would automatically be on the board of directors and act as an officer. But Corporations do not offer such fluid arrangements, offering LLCs a distinct advantage. John and Liz like this flexibility and agree to be member managers.

Manager Management

On the other hand, not every LLC wants to - or should - be managed by all of its members. An LLC with 85 members would have a difficult time getting much done at a members' management meeting. Realizing this, the framers provided that an LLC could be managed by one or more managers. Manager management may be appropriate when:

1. Certain members are investors who want no involvement or responsibility for management of the business.
2. Similarly, some members may be active in the business but don't want to be considered a "manager."
3. The owners hire an outside management professional to run the business.

4. A nonmember financier is willing to lend money but wants a say as a manager in how the money is spent.
5. Like the general partner of an LP, a member may want to manage the business as he gifts member interests to non-managing family members.

Case Number 3 – Mike and Amy

Mike and Amy are movie producers. They have produced some of the greatest low budget films of all time. Each movie has the common elements of cheerleaders, motorcycles, misunderstood psychos and at least one nerd. Mike and Amy know their audience well, and it has made them very wealthy.

To raise money for each movie Mike and Amy use a separate LLC. They follow all the securities laws and provide the proper documentation. Each investor receives a percentage of the LLC. When profits are made they flow through the LLC directly to the investor. An issue for Mike and Amy is that each movie LLC has over 200 investors. The business can't possibly be managed by all those people. Some of their money people are as oddly strange as the psychos in their movies. (One investor was even cast as a weirdo. He was brilliant, but then he wasn't acting.) So they have to come up with a way to separate investment from management.

As such, Mike and Amy decide that their LLCs will be manager-managed. They will do the managing for all their investor members who, although they have plenty of opinions and grand artistic visions, have no experience managing a movie production.

Term

Managers serve for an indefinite term in most LLCs. Instead of holding an annual shareholders' and directors' meeting and electing directors and officers for the upcoming year as with a Corporation, unless provided otherwise in the Operating Agreement, the managers serve until the members take a vote to remove them. In smaller, more informal LLCs, the initial managers will be installed and start managing. No one will give the matter of a manager's term much thought until there is a problem and one or more of the managers must be removed.

In larger LLCs, or those in which investors have placed their money and trust in the managers, set terms for the managers may be established. The Operating Agreement may be drafted providing for, as an example, one-year terms for managers after which time the members shall review the managers' performance and hold a new election.

It should be noted that unlike certain areas of corporate law, such as directors' terms and meetings, which have a defined structure and procedure, the law of LLCs is much less formal. If you want to have terms for your managers, you can put them into your Operating Agreement. If you'd rather not bother, so be it. That's your choice. If you run into a problem with your managers, state law lets you hold a vote of all the members, and the majority wins. For many, the *laissez faire* flexibility of the LLC is one of its endearing qualities. However, as discussed throughout this book, sometimes the following of certain formalities can be a useful and productive strategy.

Voting Rights

In a manager-managed LLC the members retain certain voting rights under most state statutes. (In a member managed LLC this isn't much of an issue since all members vote on everything anyway.) Besides the right to remove and replace managers, non-managing members also have the right to:

1. Approve membership changes to the LLC.
2. Approve or deny the admission of new members.
3. Approve or deny the transfer of a membership interest to an outsider.
4. Approve fundamental changes through amendment of the Articles of Organization or Operating Agreement.

5. Approve the merger or dissolution of the LLC.

Voting Power

The number of votes each member and/or manager is allowed to exercise should be clearly set out in the Operating Agreement. If your Operating Agreement is silent on this issue, your state's statute will apply by default. Typically, state laws allocate voting power according to each member's ownership interest as represented by his or her capital contribution. Some states' default rules apply a per capita standard of one vote per member. Neither of these defaults may be right for your particular situation. Be sure to set out your own standards for voting in your Operating Agreement.

Whether the members of the LLC have a voting power based upon one vote each or a percentage of ownership, state law requires that most company matters be approved by at least a voting power majority. In addition, your Operating Agreement may be drafted so that certain key votes must be decided by a supermajority. Thus, for example, the removal of a manager may require a vote of not 51 percent but 81 percent of the voting power.

There is flexibility in the realm of manager-managed LLC decision-making as well. Although most state law default provisions provide for one vote per manager and a majority vote for all manager decisions, the Operating Agreement can be drafted to provide for different standards.

Case Number 3 – Mike and Amy

As mentioned, movie investors are an interesting class. They are drawn to a project by the hopes and dreams of Hollywood, only to learn that the reality is a group of hard-nosed businessmen involved in a crapshoot where no one is ever sure of winning. But when they do win it is huge, which keeps everyone coming back for more.

Mike and Amy find that some investors are easily upset by their inevitable disillusionment with the realities of

Hollywood, and that they tend to take it out on the managers by trying to vote them out.

Being sharp people, Mike and Amy draft the Operating Agreement to create two classes of membership interests. One class, held by Mike and Amy, is able to exclusively vote for the two managers. The other class of membership interests, held by all the other investors, has no say or vote in electing the managers. This arrangement is freely disclosed to all potential investors in the LLC's investment prospectus. No one can say they aren't aware that they can't vote for a manager.

As a result, when the investors get mad, as they sometimes do, their recourse is not to hold an election and remove the managers. Mike and Amy are the only managers and, absent a court order, that will not change. The investor recourse is to demand accounting and financial records, which Mike and Amy happily provide. They have nothing to hide. And by maintaining management control they are able to conduct the business to the benefit of all their investors.

Meetings

Another distinctive feature of the LLC format is that most states do not require LLC meetings. Unlike the corporate regime of detailed procedures for the notice and call of annual and special meetings, the LLC rules are very hands-off. Several states require meetings as a default, meaning that you can provide in your Operating Agreement for no meetings and avoid the state's requirement.

Interestingly, while no meetings are required, as mentioned above, the members are required to vote on such major issues as dissolution of the LLC, removal of managers, if allowed, and amendment of the Operating Agreement. How can members vote without holding a meeting? If allowed in the Operating Agreement, the members can register their votes informally without holding a meeting or preparing meeting minutes. In some cases, they can simply sign a consent to the action taken without the need for a meeting.

Otherwise, most states have default procedures allowing LLC members or managers to call a special meeting for the taking of votes on major issues.

As discussed throughout this book, no-meeting flexibility is not ideal. The following example illustrates why:

Case Number 4 – Eric and Sherry

Eric and Sherry operate a dry cleaning business. They have borrowed money from friends and family to open the business and formed an LLC to conduct their enterprise. Each of their investors receives an LLC membership certificate reflecting the amount of money they have invested. Their Operating Agreement does not call for annual meetings or even special meetings to decide major issues. Eric and Sherry get actively involved in running the business, and before long, several years go by without any communication with the investor/members.

One of their investors, a Mr. Beye, has put more into the LLC than he probably should have. Now, he needs his $10,000 investment back for certain upcoming medical expenses. Mr. Beye calls Eric and demands his money back. While Eric is not obligated to give an equity investment back, it is really not possible anyway, as the business is not that profitable as of yet.

Mr. Beye is furious. He calls all the other investors and alleges that Eric and Sherry are cheating them. While most know Eric and Sherry well enough to know that this is not the case, the investors are universally resentful that they have not heard from Eric and Sherry regarding the business. No meetings have ever been called to explain where the business stands or to answer investor questions.

Before long, a lawyer is retained to look into Eric and Sherry's activities. Fortunately, cooler heads prevail. Eric and Sherry are allowed to hold a meeting to answer any and all questions. Eric and Sherry borrow enough money to buy out Mr. Beye for his medical expenses.

A valuable lesson is learned. Eric and Sherry now hold an annual members' meeting every year.

The failure to hold meetings can lead to miscommunication and legal jeopardy. It is a certainty that some day some court is going to hold that the fact that regular meetings were never held, that votes on major issues were never recorded and that managers went about their business for years without reporting to the members as evidence of a lack of formality in business affairs. And who could effectively challenge a court for such a finding? Your defense of being flexible only supports the lack of formality. That court will then pierce the LLC veil and hold the managers and perhaps members personally responsible for the obligations of the LLC.

In the legal field it is said that bad facts make bad law. Courts are human, and they respond to human situations. Many judges are elected and must face the public every four or six years. In certain situations, an extreme and disturbing case (bad facts) will lead to a decision that may be appropriate in the individual case but is inapplicable to the entire field (bad law). Precedent is established, allowing for future cases to be decided in the same fashion.

This is what will happen in the area of piercing the LLC veil, and perhaps in other areas of LLC law. As has been mentioned, the LLC is a new business entity without a well-defined body of law. The opportunity for bad facts to make bad law exists.

Which brings us to the key point in all of this. Despite that fact that you may draft your Operating Agreement so that no meetings are required and despite the fact that many state laws take a hands-off attitude toward the necessity of meetings, you should make meetings a regular feature of your LLC operation. Your Operating Agreement should require the preparation and retention of meeting minutes. It should provide for notice and call of meeting procedures and detail how many members or managers must be present for a valid meeting to be conducted. In this way, you will prevent some future decision allowing the piercing of the LLC veil (and it will come) from cutting against you. At the same time, you will prevent miscommunication and misunderstanding from undermining your organization.

We shall again discuss this issue in later chapters, only because it is so important.

Limited Partnership Management

Management issues for Limited Partnerships are greatly simplified and are as follows:

1. A Limited Partnership <u>must</u> be managed by a general partner.
2. A Limited Partnership <u>cannot</u> be managed by a limited partner.

<u>Case Number 2 – Mary and Gary</u>

M & G Holdings, LP has been formed for several years now and is working well for Mary and Gary. The Limited Partnership holds their brokerage account and they are so pleased with the way it works they set up another Limited Partnership, G & M Properties, LP, to hold a four-plex apartment building they own. They are gifting Limited Partnership interests to each of their three children, thus reducing their taxable estate. They are protecting and growing their assets.

Their oldest son, Charlie, holds a Limited Partnership interest in both entities. He takes a liking to helping fix up and repair the apartment building and soon asks if he can manage it and collect the rents. This is fine with his parents for it shows he wants responsibility and using Charlie is cheaper than the management company they are currently paying.

One day Gary is casually speaking with his attorney and mentions that Charlie is handling the apartment building. The attorney comes unglued. In his legal opinion, for a limited partner to manage the property is to lose all protections afforded by the Limited Partnership, including that limited partner's limited liability. Charlie cannot be involved in the management of the property. And so, to preserve and protect their limited liability protection, Mary and Gary go back to using their old management company and loan Charlie the downpayment money so he can buy and manage his own apartment building.

While the general partner has complete authority to control, he or she must still act in the best interests of the limited partners. A fiduciary duty is owed by the general partner to the limiteds (as is true for a manager in an LLC). The general partner must not waste or dissipate partnership assets, improperly maintain the books and records of the partnership or do any other act in contravention of the Partnership Agreement. The general partner also may not confess any judgments (i.e., agree to be held liable) against the partnership or perform any act that makes it impossible to carry on the partnership's ordinary business. With absolute control comes absolute responsibility.

Most state partnership laws require that the general partner obtain the majority vote (or greater, if so set out in the Partnership Agreement) of the limited partners to (1) sell all or substantially all of the partnership's assets; (2) admit a new general partner and (3) admit, in some cases, a new limited partner. At the same time, many states allow the Partnership Agreement to eliminate the right of the limiteds to replace the general partner. As such, it is possible to have a Limited Partnership controlled by a general partner who must only call meetings to discuss the most important of matters.

Again, we cite the Nevada law that provides: "The partnership agreement may grant to all or certain identified general partners the right to vote on a per-capita or any other basis, separately or with all or any class of the limited partners, on any matter." (NRS 88.465)

It is then possible to provide for controlled management continuity for several generations through a Family Limited Partnership. By having one or more managing general partners, and designating successor managing general partners, control can be maintained. In addition, by utilizing a corporate general partner and providing for the multi-generation succession of shares, continuity can be achieved. Of course, given the complexity of some of these issues it may be appropriate to consult with your professional advisors to make sure your maximum advantage is being achieved.

For Limited Partnerships, when considering the term of a general partner, voting rights and voting powers of partners, as well as the holding of partnership meetings, it is important to remember that these issues are left up to you to be drafted into the Partnership Agreement. Decide what you want and then get it down in writing into the Partnership Agreement.

Frequently Asked Questions

Can an LLC/LP have corporate-style officers?

Yes, an LLC/LP can have corporate-style officers. Having a business card that reads "Manager" or "General Partner" does not carry the weight in today's business world as does "President" or "Chief Executive Officer." These titles and lesser ones such as chief operating officer and chief financial officer, may be given to individuals working for the business.

However, you must be careful how you handle these titles. In the LLC scenario, clear lines must be established as to who can obligate the business.

In the LP scenario, the better practice is to use a corporate general partner to manage the Limited Partnership. The corporate titles (president, etc.) flow from the corporate general partner, who has traditional corporate authority to conduct the Limited Partnership's business.

Who has the authority to bind the LLC/LP?

LLC: In a member-managed LLC, each member has the authority to sign contracts that bind the LLC. In a manager-managed LLC, unless other members have been authorized, only the managers may bind the LLC.

LP: Only general partners may bind the LP.

Must LLCs/LPs maintain company records?

The general rule for most states (and a good idea anyway) is that each entity must keep the following records and, upon reasonable notice, make them available to members/limited partners.

1. All entity documents (Operating or Partnership Agreement, minutes of meetings).
2. A current list of members/partners with their addresses.
3. Voting right information.
4. All tax filings (federal, state and local).
5. Financial information including that information found on a balance sheet.

Are limiteds/members entitled to view company records?

Yes, limiteds/members are entitled to view company records. Most states provide that certain company documentation and financial information may be reviewed upon reasonable notice.

What is the fiduciary duty of care owed by a general partner/manager?

Fiduciary duty means the legal duty of general partners and managers to make business decisions, spend the entity's money and act in what they reasonably believe to be the best interests of their business. A fiduciary has a duty to act in good faith and with the utmost of care. General partners and managers, respectively, have a fiduciary duty to their limiteds and members.

What can occur if the general partner/manager breaches his or her fiduciary duty?

The limited partners/members may obtain damages from the general partner/manager if he or she breaches his or her fiduciary duty. In addition, if a majority consent was not obtained, a general partner/manager may be required to return any profits or benefits received from taking an opportunity that was the company's to pursue.

Who can act as a manager/general partner?

LLC: Most states allow any person (United States or foreign national), Corporation, partnership, Trust, or separate LLC to serve as manager. But check your state rules, which may be subject to change. Colorado requires a natural person, 18 years or older. Minnesota requires an 18 year old or older individual, disallowing Corporations and the like.

LP: Again, most states allow individuals, Corporations, LLCs and Trusts to serve as general partners. Be sure to check your state's statute for any variance to this general rule.

Must a general partner/manager be a partner/member?

LLC: If an LLC is member-managed, by definition, the managers must be members. In a manager-managed scenario, however, a manager does not have to be a member. As previously discussed, in some LLCs the members will bring in a professional (nonmember) manager to run the business.

LP: As a general rule, a general partner should be a partner and have a partnership interest in the Limited Partnership. While certain creative arrangements can be made whereby a general partner has a lesser form of partnership interest, be sure to consult with your professional advisor on how (and why) to craft such a strategy.

Who elects the initial general partner(s)/manager(s)?

The initial general partner(s)/manager(s) must be named in the certificate of Limited Partnership/Articles of Organization filed with the state. So they must be agreed upon and appointed by the founding partners/members at the very first meeting.

Must the general partner(s)/manager(s) be residents of the state of entity formation?

No, unless such requirement is set forth in the Partnership Agreement or the Operating Agreement, general partner(s)/manager(s) need not be residents of the state of entity formation.

Does an LP/LLC have to hold regular meetings for its limited partners/members?

Though not necessary, as a practical matter, as discussed throughout the book, the better practice is to hold an annual meeting.

Are general partner(s)/manager(s) required to be elected on an annual basis?

LLC: Most states allow the members to set up their own procedures for the election of managers, which may be annual or otherwise. A few states, unless agreed to the contrary by the members, require the annual election of managers.

LP: No, unless so required in the Partnership Agreement, general partner(s) need not be elected on an annual basis.

Can the limited partner(s)/member(s) remove a general partner/manager with or without cause?

LLC: Again, it depends on what is provided in the Operating Agreement. If the Operating Agreement is silent on the issue, the default rules of each state's statute apply. These rules differ from state to state. The better practice, once again, is to draft exactly the procedure you want into the Agreement.

LP: It depends on what is provided for in the Partnership Agreement. If the agreement is so drafted, removal with or without cause can be accomplished. If the agreement is silent, state law will apply, and on this issue, each state's law is different. The better practice is to draft the agreement with the procedure you want in place.

Can a manager/general partner be indemnified and held harmless for claims that may arise?

Yes, with both entities, indemnification is an option. But check whether your state statute limits the extent of any indemnification.

When can a limited partner become liable as a general partner?

When a limited becomes actively involved in the business and its management, liability may attach. Nevada's law on this issue is well drafted and protects the limiteds as best as possible. It states:

> "1. Except as provided in subsection 4, a limited partner is not liable for the obligations of a limited partnership unless he is also a general partner or, in addition to the exercise of his rights and powers as a limited partner, he participates in the control of the business. However, if the limited partner participates in the control of the business, he is

liable only to persons who transact business with the limited partnership reasonably believing, based upon the limited partner's conduct, that he is a general partner.

2. A limited partner does not participate in the control of the business within the meaning of subsection 1 solely by doing one or more of the following:

(a) Being a contractor for an agent or employee of the limited partnership or of a general partner or being an officer, director or shareholder of a general partner that is a corporation;

(b) Consulting with or advising a general partner with respect to the business of the limited partnership;

(c) Acting as a surety for the limited partnership by guaranteeing or assuming one or more specific obligations of the limited partnership'

(d) Taking any action required or permitted by law to bring or pursue a derivative action in the right of the limited partnership;

(e) Requesting or attending a meeting of the partners;

(f) Proposing, approving or disapproving, by voting or otherwise, one or more of the following matters:

(1) The dissolution and winding up of the limited partnership;

(2) The sale, exchange, lease, mortgage, pledge or other transfer of all or substantially all of the assets of the limited partnership;

(3) The incurrence of indebtedness by the limited partnership other than in the ordinary course of business;

(4) A change in the nature of the business;

(5) The admission or removal of a general partner;

(6) The admission or removal of a limited partner;

(7) A transaction involving an actual or potential conflict of interest between a general partner and the limited partnership or limited partners;

(8) An amendment to the partnership agreement or certificate of limited partnership;

(9) Matters related to the business of the limited partnership not otherwise enumerated in this subsection, which the partnership agreement states in writing may be subject to the approval or disapproval of limited partners;

(g) Winding up the limited partnership pursuant to NRS 88.560; or

(h) Exercising any right or power permitted to limited partners under this chapter and not specifically enumerated in this subsection.

3. The enumeration in subsection 2 does not mean that the possession or exercise of any other powers by a limited partner constitutes participation by him in the business of the limited partnership.

4. A limited partner who knowingly permits his name to be used in the name of the limited partnership, except under circumstances permitted by paragraph (b) of subsection 1 of NRS 88.320, is liable to creditors who extend credit to the limited partnership without actual knowledge that the limited partner is not a general partner." (NRS 88.430)

Nevertheless, as noted above, where a limited acts as a general he or she may be personally liable to creditors. The key to avoiding such a fate is to not tempt it. If you are a limited partner, do not act as a general partner.

What LP/LLC decisions require unanimous agreement?

As previously mentioned, approval of the Limited Partnership/Operating Agreement requires unanimous consent in many states. The better practice is to have each partner/member sign the agreement, thereby agreeing to be bound by its terms. Some states require that amending the agreements also require a unanimous vote. Again, it is good practice to have each partner/member sign any amended agreement. Other decisions, by prior agreement, may be required to have a unanimous vote.

Is there any set standard for how much should or can be paid in management fees to a general partner/manager?

There is no set standard for management compensation. Please note that the federal government wants to see a reasonable salary being paid whenever possible so that payroll taxes may be assessed, in order to forestall the coming bankruptcy of the Social Security System. Factors to be considered in arriving at a reasonable amount will include the gross revenue of the LP/LLC, the level of management services rendered and comparable industry standards for compensation. A good accountant can help you to arrive at the right number, or you can visit www.salary.com.

Chapter Four
Entity Taxation

All right, I told you it was coming. I know just the thought of taxes gets the blood boiling for some of you. And for the rest of you, the time and trouble it takes just to compile the darn paperwork constitutes one of life's major annoyances.

But we'll get through it quickly and efficiently. You'll receive enough information to understand the landscape and, hopefully, be able to sit down with your accountant and map out your strategy. We'll briefly review certain LP and LLC, as well as Corporation, Sole Proprietorship and General Partnership tax information to help you make informed decisions as to which entity is right for you.

Sole Proprietors and Single-Member LLCs

For Sole Proprietorships and single-member (one person) LLCs the tax reporting requirements are very basic. You do not have to prepare or file any additional tax returns. You simply attach a Schedule C, Profit or Loss from a Business (or other schedule, if applicable), to your Form 1040 individual return. On the Schedule C you will detail your profits or losses from your Sole Proprietorship or single-member LLC.

In addition, Sole Proprietor and single-members of an LLC will file a Schedule SE, Self-Employment Tax Return with their Form 1040. On this schedule you will calculate the amount of self-employment tax (Social Security and Medicare) owed. Currently, the self-employment tax is 12.4 percent for Social Security on earnings up to a statutory maximum of $87,900 for 2004, and 2.9 percent for Medicare. You may deduct half of the self-employment tax from your income before you pay your personal income tax. All monies flowing through your Sole Proprietorship or single-member LLC will be subject to self-employment tax.

Although more fully discussed below, it should be noted here that limited partners, Sub-Chapter S Corporation shareholders and members without active participation in an LLC do not have to pay self-employment taxes on allocated profits. This can be a useful planning strategy.

General Partnerships, Limited Partnerships and Multi-Member LLCs

For flow-through tax entities with two or more owners, the tax filing is somewhat more involved. As a reminder, you must have two partners to form a General Partnership. You must have at least one general and one limited partner to form a Limited Partnership. And, although an LLC may have only one member, when two or more members are involved, the LLC generally files its taxes like a partnership.

If you are involved in any of the three above-mentioned entities you will be required to prepare and file an IRS Form 1065, United States Partnership Return of Income. Since the entity itself does not pay any tax, it is called an informational return. But the information required may require the assistance of a bookkeeper or accountant, or at least a good software program. Form 1065 imposes the necessity of double entry bookkeeping with a journal of accounts posted to a general ledger. From the general ledger an income statement and balance sheet are prepared and used to complete the tax return. Form 1065 will detail each owner's capital account, including capital contributions, distributions and allocations and distributions of profits.

Income, losses, deductions and credits allocated to each owner for the year are reported on Schedule K of Form 1065. A Schedule K-1 is then given to each owner with his or her own specific distributive share of profits, losses, deductions and credits for the year posted. Included in this schedule are certain specialized types of income and deductions such as short-term and long-term capital gains and losses, foreign taxes paid, taxable and tax-exempt interest, medical expenses and alternative minimum tax preference items. As an owner, you attach a K-1 to your Form 1040 and use it to calculate the amount of personal income tax owed. A brief example is instructive.

Case Number 1 – John and Liz

J & L Consulting, LLC has a very good first year. They have consulted with clients in eight western states, five southeastern states, three northeastern states and two Canadian maritime provinces. John and Liz are both busy and pleased that they have left their large corporate jobs for the challenge of their own business.

Their income statement for December 31st of this year is as follows:

LLC (or Partnership) Item	Income Statement	Net Income	Separately Stated
Sales	500,000	500,000	
Operating Expenses	(300,000)	(300,000)	
State and Local Taxes	(25,000)	(25,000)	
Foreign Taxes	(2,000)		(2,000)
Dividends	3,000		3,000
Taxable Interest	2,500		2,500
Tax Exempt Interest	1,000		1,000
Short-Term Capital Gains	1,000		1,000
Long-Term Capital Losses	(1,000)		(1,000)
	179,500	175,000	4,500

As such, John and Liz, being equal members in the LLC, will receive a K-1 listing their share of income as follows:

LLC (or Partnership) Item	Income Statement	John	Liz
Ordinary Net Income	$175,000	$87,500	$87,500
Foreign Taxes	(2,000)	(1,000)	(1,000)
Dividends	3,000	1,500	1,500
Taxable Interest	2,500	1,250	1,250
Tax-exempt interest	1,000	500	500
Short-Term Capital Gains	1,000	500	500
Long-Term Capital Losses	(1,000)	(500)	(500)
	$179,500	$89,750	$89,750

This is the same flow-through tax treatment that John and Liz would have received if they had operated as a General Partnership. The advantage, of course, of an LLC over a General Partnership is that John and Liz, by operating as an LLC, have protected their personal assets. They have obtained the same beneficial flow-through taxation of a General Partnership without the unwanted unlimited personal exposure of a General Partnership.

Allocations

As discussed, a unique feature of the LLC is the ability of its members to split profits and losses disproportionate to capital contributions and ownership interests. For example, an LLC can provide 40 percent of the profits to a member who only contributed 20 percent of the initial capital. This is achieved by making a special allocation.

To be accepted by the IRS, special allocations must have a "substantial economic effect." In IRS lingo this means that the allocation must be based upon legitimate economic circumstances. An allocation cannot be used to simply reduce one owner's tax obligations.

Let's say that John, as an inducement to enter into the LLC, is granted a 15 percent return on his initial investment. After his 15 percent return, the members will share equally in the profit from operations. Because John is able to get the economic benefit of the 15 percent return on his investment, allocating sufficient profit to John to cover the priority return, the IRS will respect the allocation. The substantial economic effect rules will not be violated if the dollars follow the allocation.

By including special language in your LLC's Operating Agreement you may be able to create a safe harbor to insure that future special allocations will have a substantial economic effect. As with ships at sea, a safe harbor for IRS purposes is a place of comfort and certainty.

The required language deals with the following:

1. Capital accounts. Each member's capital account must be carried on the books under special rules set forth in the IRS regulations. Consult with your tax advisor on these rules. They are not unusual or out of the ordinary.
2. Liquidation based upon capital accounts. Upon dissolution of the LLC, distributions are to be made according to positive capital account balances.
3. Negative capital account paybacks. Any members with a negative capital account balance must return their account to a zero balance upon the sale or liquidation of the LLC, or when the owner sells his interest.

It should be noted that complying with the special allocation rules and qualifying under the safe harbor provisions is a complicated area of the law. Be sure to consult with an advisor who is qualified to assist you in this arena.

Sub-Chapter S Corporations

Once the Form 2553 for a Sub-Chapter S Corporation is filed with the IRS and the IRS accepts it, the Sub-Chapter S Corporation will be taxed as a flow-through entity. Profits and losses will pass through the Corporation and be reported on the shareholder's individual tax returns. This is the same tax treatment that the owners of partnerships and LLCs receive.

Remember, however, that in an LLC, profits and losses can be allocated according to factors separate and independent of percentage ownership interest. In an S Corporation, on the other hand, shareholders may only be allocated such distributions according to their share of ownership.

Still, there are certain advantages to using a Sub-Chapter S Corporation. A working owner of a highly profitable business may want to consider using a Sub-Chapter S Corporation. As long as he or she declares a salary that is reasonable and customary for his or her industry, and pays employment taxes on that amount, the remainder of his or her income stream may flow through as profits without the need to pay additional self-employment taxes. This can represent a major tax savings over other entities, including LLCs. But again, remember there is no one right answer in all of this. You need to work with your advisors to come up with what is best for you.

C Corporations

C Corporations require a corporate tax return on IRS Form 1120, Corporate Income Tax Return. Unlike the entities discussed above, a C Corporation pays its own income taxes on any profits left in the company at the end of the year. If after the payment of corporate taxes the company wants to benefit its shareholders, it may use after-tax profits to distribute dividends to the shareholders. However, the shareholders must pay tax on the dividends received – thus the notion of a double-tax, first on corporate profits and then on shareholder dividends. This double-tax can be minimized with proper planning. Also note that the Corporation's owners will also pay taxes at their own particular individual tax rate on any salaries and bonuses they have received throughout the year.

Nonetheless, a unique advantage of C Corporations is that the initial tax rates are generally lower than a shareholder's individual tax rates. For up to $50,000 in corporate profits, the tax rate at the time of this writing is just 15 percent, and it is 25 percent on the next $25,000 in profits.

For a business that needs to retain profits in the company for expansion or other reasons in the upcoming year, the advantage of not flowing year-end profits through the business to the owners can be significant. In a moment we will discuss how an LLC can accomplish this tax treatment.

Another issue minimizing the specter of C Corporation double taxation is that a Corporation may provide the best exit strategy in many cases. If the owners, for example, see going public as their grand reward, a C Corporation will have to be used.

Issues Facing All LPs, LLCs, SPs and GPs

In flow-through entities, the owners pay individual income taxes on all net profits of the business. This is the case whether they receive those net profits or not.

For example, assume an LLC or a partnership business has three equal owners/managers and it nets $300,000 for the year. Each owner must report a gain of $100,000 and pay individual income taxes on that amount. But what if the business needs that $300,000 to expand into a new market or acquire new equipment for the upcoming year?

Assuming the partners are all in the highest 35 percent (at the time of this writing) individual tax bracket and are all active in management (thus requiring the payment of 15.3 percent in self employment taxes), just over half of the amount allocated to each will be due in taxes. But if the business needs to retain the money for the upcoming year and does not distribute any of it, each partner must come up with over $50,000 out of pocket to satisfy the tax obligation on their $100,000 allocated but undistributed gain. It is not realistic to think that many owners would choose this course of action.

The situation in which an owner is allocated a gain without the receipt of any money is known as phantom income. The appearance of income on your tax return is all the IRS wants or needs. How you get the money in reality to pay the tax is not its concern. In Chapter Seven we discuss how phantom income can be used to your asset protection advantage. For now, suffice it to say, the current example of phantom income is not advantageous to owners.

In some cases, the owners of the entity will choose to distribute enough money so that the partners may at least satisfy their tax obligations. This is frequently the case in investment Limited Partnerships that manage real property or other assets. While money may be needed for improvements to property and deferred maintenance, the general partners are wise enough to distribute just enough money for the limiteds to cover their tax bills. There is no greater cause of turmoil and general partner removal in a Limited Partnership than the allocation of phantom income to the limiteds. Furthermore, the Operating Agreement of an LLC or the Partnership Agreement of a partnership may require the distributions of money in order to cover taxes.

In the example above, with a $100,000 gain to each partner of the active business, the entity could distribute $50,000 to each limited to pay income and self-employment taxes. But then what happens to the reserve for expansion, equipment or future business needs? It is reduced from $300,000 to $150,000. This is not an ideal situation. In fact, the partners would be better off under corporate taxation.

Flow-Through Entities Taxed As Corporations

The IRS recently acknowledged the above-mentioned problem and made it allowable for LLCs and partnerships to become taxed as Corporations. It should be noted that in prior years, owners of LLCs and partnerships with the need to retain, instead of distribute, profits to meet future business needs were forced to actually convert their business into a Corporation to be taxed as one. Now you have the option of retaining your existing LLC or partnership structure and yet be taxed as a Corporation. The advantage to LLC and partnership owners is that they can now pay individual income taxes on only the profits actually paid to them. The business then pays taxes on any retained profits at the reduced corporate tax rates.

To elect corporate tax treatment you must file IRS Form 8832, Entity Classification Election, with the IRS. Either an authorized member or all members sign the form. Copies of any authorization for one member to sign the form, as well as a copy of the form itself, should be kept with the partnership or LLC records.

The election takes effect on a date you select and place on Form 8832. This date cannot be 12 months after or 75 days before you file the form. Failure to specify a date results in the election becoming effective on the date the form is received by the IRS. In the first year of filing corporate returns, the LLC or partnership must include a copy of Form 8832 with its corporate tax return.

You should carefully consider whether or not to seek a corporate tax election. Certainly, you should consult with your accountant or professional advisor before filing for such an election. A significant reason for caution is that once the election is made you cannot return to flow-through taxation for a period of five years. If you foresee profitability for the next five years and the need to retain earnings, the election probably makes sense. Still, it is advisable to consult with your advisor on this issue.

In addition to the business being taxed as a Corporation, owner(s)/manager(s) who work for the business will, in essence, become corporate employees. They will become subject to the withholding of payroll, self-employment and unemployment taxes in the same way that other non-owner employees of a partnership or LLC are.

It should be noted that when an LLC or partnership elects to be treated as a Corporation for tax purposes it does not become one in a legal sense. The state statutes on LLCs and partnerships will still govern operations. The owners and investors will still hold membership or partnership interests as opposed to corporate stock. Above all, in your dealings with the public you will still designate yourself as an LLC or partnership, not as a Corporation.

Self-Employment Taxes

The Federal Self-Employment Tax is a Social Security and Medicare tax for individuals who work for themselves. It is just like the tax for Social Security and Medicare that is withheld from the paychecks of wage earners. Unlike other forms of doing business, all net earnings from self-employment are subject to this tax. As such, on any and all earnings below a statutory maximum of $87,900 (in 2004), whether classified as salary or profit, self-employed individuals will pay a 15.3 percent tax. Earnings above the statutory maximum continue to be subject to Medicare tax at the rate of 2.9 percent.

As mentioned above, after paying employment taxes on any salaries earned, the use of certain entities such as Limited Partnerships and Sub-Chapter S Corporations will obviate the need to pay the self-employment tax on all monies flowing through the business. Those entities that are not engaged in a trade or business, but are rather limited to very passive investments such as asset holdings, will also not be subject to self-employment taxation. Consult with your tax professional as to whether your entity is engaged in a trade or business or not. For those engaged in a trade or business, the following applies:

In a Limited Partnership, an individual limited partner's distributive share of partnership income is not considered self-employment income unless that person receives guaranteed payments for services rendered to the partnership. An individual general partner of a Limited Partnership will be subject to the Federal Self-Employment Tax on his or her distributive share of ordinary income from the Limited Partnership's trade or business and receipt of any guaranteed payments for services rendered to the partnership. However, a general partner's share of rental income from real estate held for investment is not considered self-employment income.

It is important to remember that self-employment taxes are based on the partner's distributive share, whether distributed or not. Yes, the phantom of income strikes again. Not only will you pay income tax on the money you don't receive but, if applicable, self- employment taxes as well.

With regard to the certainty of death and taxes, when a partner whose income is subject to self-employment tax passes away, the year is prorated. The amount treated as self-employment income will be his or her distributive share up to the first day of the first month following his or her death.

It should be noted that many Limited Partnerships are structured so that the limiteds own, for example, 98 percent of the partnership and the general only owns 2 percent. In certain situations, one individual will be both a general partner and a limited partner of the same Limited Partnership. In that case, unless guaranteed payments for services are made to him or her as a limited partner, self-employment tax will only be due on the individual general partner's distributive share. And even if the general is not a limited, the amount due for self-employment income in all cases is generally minimized because the general partner owns such a small percentage of the Limited Partnership. If $100,000 from trade or business activities flows through the Limited Partnership, only the general partner is subject to self-employment taxes. In the scenario above, with the general partner owning 2 percent of the Limited Partnership, the self-employment tax will be paid on $2,000 of income.

A strategy to consider is to have a C Corporation serve as the general partner of the Limited Partnership or as the manager of an LLC. Any management fee collected as the general partner or manager does not constitute self-employment earnings. Any compensation paid to officers and directors would be subject to ordinary income tax, but income taxes can be eliminated by having the officers and directors serve without compensation. However, the C Corporation can set up health care insurance and a medical reimbursement plan, and all of the officers and directors (and their spouses) can be covered under the plan. Health care and medical reimbursement coverage are deductible by the C Corporation and are not considered income to the officers and directors for tax purposes.

Medical Expenses

Unless the owner of a pass-through entity has medical expenses that exceed 7½ percent of their adjusted gross income (the IRS makes this near impossible) so as to itemize their medical expenses, in order to deduct 100 percent of the cost, only a portion of medical expenses can be deducted on the individual tax return. As of 2003, a full deduction of health premiums is available for all entities. See your tax advisor as to where such deductions are taken on your tax returns.

Employee Fringe Benefits

Group life and disability insurance, qualified employee retirement plans and similar fringe benefits may be deducted as business expenses by a C Corporation. The Corporation's owners and employees receiving these benefits are not taxed on their individual returns for the value of such benefits. On the other hand, in flow-through entities the owners must pay taxes on the value of the benefits received.

In addition, the fringe benefit discrimination rules tend to prevent the owners of Sub-Chapter S Corporations and LLC members from receiving the maximum tax benefit of certain fringe benefit packages. By contrast, no C Corporation employee is excluded from access to fringe benefits because he or she is also a shareholder of that C Corporation.

In the area of qualified benefit plans, C Corporations hold the following advantages:

1. Corporate owners can receive tax-free term life (within limits) and medical benefits.
2. Contributions to plans may create a net operating loss for the business.
3. Corporate owners may borrow from the retirement plan.

Nevertheless, the issue of fringe benefits is not going to be a deciding factor for many new or smaller businesses. The expense of implementing and consistently funding an elaborate benefits package is beyond the means of many companies.

Taxation on Appreciation

Members of an LLC are not exposed to double taxation on the increased value of company assets upon the dissolution of the LLC. This is because the LLC's tax liabilities pass through the entity to the LLC members. Therefore, the LLC, unlike a Corporation, does not pay a tax on any appreciation of its assets.

In addition, a transfer to a Sub-Chapter S Corporation of appreciated property in exchange for shares will be a taxable event unless after the transfer the transferors own at least 80 percent of the voting stock and only receive stock (not cash or other consideration) in the deal. On the other hand, transferring appreciated property into an LLC in exchange for membership interests will not be taxed unless liabilities are also being transferred into the LLC and the liabilities being transferred in exceed the combined total of the transferor's share of the LLC's liabilities and the basis of the property being contributed.

If it is anticipated that post formation contributions are going to be made to an entity, it would be advisable to use an LLC instead of an S Corporation.

Adjustments to Partnership Basis Upon Death

A general rule of partnership taxation is that a partnership or LLC has one tax basis in its assets (known as the "inside basis") and the partner/members have a separate tax basis in their ownership interests (called the "outside basis").

When all the partners acquire their ownership interests through the contribution of capital, their outside basis will line up with the entity's inside basis. If each of four partners puts up $5,000 each, the inside and outside basis will be the same.

Instead, if a new partner acquires an interest through a later purchase or exchange or by succession due to the death of a prior partner, the new partner's outside basis will be different than his or her pro rata share of the entity's inside basis. This occurs most frequently upon the death of a partner, as under federal tax law there is an automatic step up in the value of the outside basis to the date of death value of the partnership interest. There is not a corresponding step up of the partnership's inside basis unless an election is made pursuant to Section 754.

Case Number 5 - Mario, Victor, Jerry and Vinny

Mario, Victor and Jerry are equal members of an LLC that holds real property with a purchase price basis of $30,000 and a fair market value of $150,000. Jerry passes away and leaves his one-third interest to his cousin Vinny. Under IRS Section 1014, Vinny receives a stepped up basis valued at the date of death, of $50,000 (one-third of the $150,000 fair market value). With a Section 754 election in place, Vinny's inside basis is also stepped up from $10,000 (one-third of the $30,000 purchase price basis) to $50,000. If the LLC later sells the property for $50,000, Vinny has no gain, unless the property is later depreciated.

Under Section 754 a reduction in basis can also occur. If in the previous example the basis were still $30,000 but the fair market value was $15,000, Vinny's basis would be reduced from $10,000 to $5,000.

Also of note, a 754 basis step up is depreciable by Vinny. To be effective a Section 754 election must include the name and address of the electing LLC or partnership and be signed by one of the partners/members. While available to LLCs and partnerships, Section 754 elections may not be used by Sub-Chapter S Corporations.

Tax Basis of Debt

An advantage LLCs have over Limited Partnerships and S Corporations has to do with the tax basis of business debt. In a Sub-Chapter S Corporation, business debts do not increase a shareholder's tax basis for taking losses. Only direct loans to the Sub-Chapter S Corporation from a shareholder can add to that shareholder's "at risk" amount. In a Limited Partnership, liability for which one or more of the partners bears the risk of loss, or recourse liability, is only included in the partner's outside basis in proportion to the respective obligation to discharge the liability. Further, nonrecourse liability, where no partner bears an economic risk, is allocated to the partners according to their respective profit interests.

Let's say that an LLC has a loss of $12,000 in the first year of operations. The two members each contributed $2,500 to initially fund the LLC. Additionally, the LLC secured a line of credit for $7,000. In order to get the line, each partner personally guaranteed the debt. The entire $12,000 loss would flow through to the LLC members, and they would have sufficient basis to deduct the loss on their personal income tax returns. If this same structure existed in a Sub-Chapter S Corporation, the shareholder would not have sufficient basis to deduct the loss because he or she would only get basis for debt that he or she had directly with the entity.

Tax on Distributions

Both a member of an LLC and an S Corporation shareholder recognize gain to the extent that a distribution of money exceeds his or her adjusted basis in his or her interest.

However, if appreciated property is distributed from an S Corporation, the gain is recognized on distribution as if it were sold. On the other hand, if the LLC distributed the same property, no gain would be recognized, and the distributed property would receive a carryover basis in the hands of the members.

For example, assume JoeBob LLC has one asset. It is a 1950 single-wide mobile home that has been rented for years to MarySue. It has an adjusted basis in the LLC of $500 and a fair market value of $4,500. Joe and Bob (the two owners of the LLC) want to discontinue the LLC and get out of the rental real estate business. Because the mobile home is owned in an LLC, the LLC can evict the tenant and distribute the property to the members without a tax consequence. The basis in the mobile home that is distributed will be $500. Joe and Bob could then occupy the mobile home without a tax consequence.

If the mobile home were in an S Corporation, the $4,000 of appreciation would be recognized as gain and reported on the shareholders' income tax returns. This would be a substantial cost of terminating business to Joe and Bob. This example represents another good reason why real estate is better held in an LLC (or an LP) instead of within an S Corporation.

Tax Free Combinations

A very clear advantage that S Corporations have over LLCs and LPs is the ability of S Corporations and their shareholders to utilize the tax-free entity reorganization rules. There are no such rules for LPs and LLCs that allow for the participation in tax-free reorganizations and mergers.

Thus, for shareholders, the exchange of stock in their Corporation for the stock in a Corporation that is a party to the reorganization will generally be tax-free. In an LP or LLC a termination may occur if greater than 50 percent of the ownership changes within a year. Such reorganization or merger may also trigger a taxable event depending on the circumstances. Be sure to check with your accountant before proceeding in this area.

And speaking of accountants, the two excellent professionals who helped me with this section indicated that to answer the following questions in full CPA detail would take up another book. So, the answers are intentionally brief and the point is underscored that it makes sense to have a good accountant on your team to assist with the complexities of partnership tax law.

Frequently Asked Questions

What are the "check the box" regulations?

Entities that have two or more members/partners are taxed as partnerships, and entities with one member will be disregarded (but will also have flow-through taxation). Under the "check the box" regulations, a flow-through entity may elect to be taxed as a Corporation.

What is a tax matters member or partner?

A tax matters member/partner is a designated person to represent the partnership before the IRS.

What are capital accounts?

A capital account represents a partner or member's undistributed ownership balance.

What is the difference between a capital account and tax basis?

A capital account reflects the partner/member's economic book value. Tax basis represents the partner/member's holding value.

What is the capital account of a partner/member who acquires his or her interest from another partner/member?

The capital account, in this case, is the selling partner/member's inside basis.

What are the tax consequences upon selling an LLC/LP interest?

Generally, it is a capital gain unless the sale triggers a termination, which can then involve a greater tax depending upon the facts and circumstances associated with the underlying assets.

Do the controlled group status rules that apply to C Corporations apply to LPs, LLCs and Sub-Chapter S Corporations as well?

Yes, the rules are the same for all. Even if you only have one C Corporation the IRS Section 179 expense election, for example, applies to all entities.

Is a member/partner taxed on services rendered in exchange for an entity interest?

Yes, services rendered are taxed when exchanged for an ownership interest in an entity.

Must a gain be recognized when a member/partner contributes appreciated property to the entity?

Generally, no, a gain need not be recognized.

Can a loss be recognized on the contribution of property?

No, a loss cannot be recognized on a property contribution.

Are distributions to a member/partner from an LP or LLC taxable?

Generally distributions such as this are not taxable, since the entity annually passes its tax implications in the K-1 report to the member/partner. A mere distribution of cash does not create a taxable event unless the member/partner has a negative capital account. Distributions of property can be more complex depending on the nature of the property and the underlying circumstances.

How can the entity deduct formation expenses?

The entity can elect to amortize formation expenses over sixty months.

Can an LP/LLC use either a cash or accrual basis for accounting?

Yes, although in some cases an accrual basis is mandatory.

Can new partners/members receive income and losses accrued by the LLC prior to their admittance?

No, claimed income and losses can only be for the period after new partners/members are admitted to the LLC..

Are there limits to the amount of entity losses that can be used to offset a member or partner's other income?

Yes, there are limits, particularly in the area of passive activity rules. (Passive income is income you receive but didn't directly do anything to earn. For example, interest on your savings account or dividends received on stock you hold in a company are considered passive income.)

Is there ever a time when limited partners could receive non-passive (active) income from a Limited Partnership?

Yes, if a limited partner receives a guaranteed payment for services (versus capital), non-passive, or active, income may be generated on which employment taxes may be assessed. But remember, limited partners technically should not perform services for an LP.

How do the at-risk rules apply to members/partners?

The deduction of losses is limited to the amount determined to be at risk.

Do the passive/active loss rules apply to members/partners?

Yes, passive/active loss rules apply.

Upon the sale of an LLC/LP entity what are the tax consequences?

It can be a taxable event as determined by partnership tax law. Generally, if the partnership has any "hot assets" (as defined by Internal Revenue Code ("IRC") section 751), the gain on the sale of a partnership will be ordinary to the extent of gain attributable to these assets. Section 751 assets are inventory and other assets that would result in ordinary income if they were sold in the partnership. These are typically assets that were depreciated using accelerated depreciation.

Upon termination or liquidation of an LLC/LP what are the tax consequences?

The tax attributes of a termination or liquidation are determined by partnership tax law. The basis of the distributed property is the basis to the partnership plus any gain recognized on the distribution. Gain will be recognized only if cash or cash equivalents are distributed and exceed the basis in the partnership.

What are the tax consequences of merging or converting a Corporation to an LLC/LP?

There are potential built-in taxes with the merging or converting of a Corporation to an LLC/LP.

What are the special tax issues involved with a California LLC?

1. California assesses extra fees for using an LLC. The extra fee for the year 2003 was:

If total annual income is Equal to or over -	But not over -	The fee is:
$ 250,000	$ 499,999	$ 900
500,000	999,999	2,500
1,000,000	4,999,999	6,000
5,000,000	And over	11,790

To determine the LLC fee, "total income" means gross income plus the cost of goods sold connected with the LLC's trade or business, or, essentially, gross revenue.

2. The pass-through of California income to non-California residents requires the filing of a State of California tax return and the payment of California taxes.

Who selects the entity's tax year?

The tax year (the accounting period for tax reporting) must conform to the partners' tax year as follows:

1. If one or more partners own more than 50 percent in interest and have the same tax year, that tax year must be used.
2. If there is no majority interest, the tax year must be that of the majority of principal partners (those that own 5 percent or more in interest.) Remember, all United States individual tax years end on December 31st. The issue comes up when Corporations or other entities (which may have non-calendar year tax years) are involved.

What is a hybrid LLC?

An LLC that is classified as a partnership in one country and a Corporation in another is a hybrid LLC. This designation is used in international business transactions to take advantage of the tax laws of different countries.

Can an LLC/LP interest qualify for IRS Section 1244 treatment?

No, an LLC/LP interest does not qualify. Section 1244 allows for ordinary income losses (as opposed to capital losses) on certain qualified small business corporations. This provision only applies to Corporations, not LLCs or LPs.

Chapter Five

Capital Contributions, Ownership and the Securities Laws

Once an LLC/LP is formed it most often needs to be financed. Raising money for any entity involves complying with the securities laws. A good overview of the entire securities area can be found in *How Your Company Can Raise Money to Grow and Go Public*, by Robert Paul Turner and Megan Hughes (Success DNA, 2001). But for now, a brief understanding of the securities laws is important.

The most common method of financing is to sell ownership interests to persons who want to be members or partners. In some cases entities are financed with debt or with a combination of debt and equity. Contributions can consist of cash, services rendered or agreed to be provided, promissory notes and/or property. (Please note that some states do not allow future promises, such as a promissory note, to serve as consideration for acquiring an interest). The company's organizational documents should specify the procedures for financing and issuing ownership interests and the amount of contributions to be received.

Case Number 3 – Mike and Amy

Our movie producers are savvy about putting together film investment deals. In the early 80s they used Limited Partnerships for the huge upfront tax losses they could generate. When all those tax shelters were swiftly eliminated by the Tax Reform Act of 1986, and investors were financially slaughtered for using what had once been a legal tax vehicle, Mike and Amy sat on the sidelines for a few years amid the resulting turmoil. Then they learned of the Wyoming LLC, and that many states were following it with their own LLC legislation.

Whereas bitter and battered investors did not want to even hear the words "Limited Partnership," a "Limited Liability

Company" was a new and fresh approach that Mike and Amy could use on investors. Granted, unlike before 1986, their film deals actually had to have investment merit and be geared to generating profits and not losses. But with an LLC they could maintain control, as they used to as general partners of a Limited Partnership, and they could sell the flow-through tax concept to their investors.

Over the years since 1986, Limited Partnerships have lost their taint and are now used again as investment entities. But Mike and Amy's experience with LPs was so dramatic they have stuck with using LLCs for their film investment deals.

So how do Mike and Amy handle an LLC film deal with their investors?

First of all, they follow all the securities laws. Failure to comply with these very important rules can lead to a great deal of trouble, including time in jail.

Mike and Amy use an investment document called a private placement memorandum (PPM) to sell interests in their film projects. They would use a similar PPM if they were selling Limited Partnership interests in a Limited Partnership.

The PPM sets out very clearly what the capital contributions are and what percentage of the company the investor will receive. The PPM ties into the Operating Agreement, which details the same investment procedure. In Mike and Amy's average film deal, in exchange for $25,000 in cash the investor gets a 1 percent interest in the LLC, which after expenses means 1 percent of the profits. These terms are carefully spelled out in the Operating Agreement and the PPM. As mentioned, an LLC (or LP) can be financed with promissory notes, property and the like. But Mike and Amy need cash to make movies and that's all they accept.

Mike and Amy know that investors like to receive a piece of paper, akin to a share certificate for a Corporation, evidencing their ownership in the LLC. While in most states certificates are not required for investors in LLCs or LPs, Mike and Amy know it is better practice and good investor relations to issue a certificate of ownership. They do put a legend on the certificate indicating that there are restrictions on transferring the interest, thus putting third parties on notice that the consent of the other members/partners is required. And, unlike before 1986, by generating real profits for their investors Mike and Amy have continued making movies.

The Relationship Between LLCs, LPs and United States Securities Laws

Although many people believe that the application of securities laws and regulations only apply to public companies, or to companies planning to go public, in truth securities laws apply to every business entity within the United States that issues any form of security, including LLC membership interests and LP Limited Partnership interests.

Securities laws are found at both the federal and the state level. The federal legislation consists of two major bodies of legislation that control the disposition, issuing, buying, selling and other transfers of securities. These two bodies of law are United States Securities Act of 1933, as amended (the 1933 Act), and the United States Securities & Exchange Act of 1934, as amended (the 1934 Act), and their respective rules and regulations. Each state also has separate securities legislation, although many of the states have adopted the Uniform Commercial Code as their governing securities authority. Business entities must ensure that they comply with both federal and state legislation; however, for the purpose of this chapter we will concentrate on how federal securities laws impact the operations of LPs and LLCs. You may want to check with your legal advisor as to state securities issues.

Although the stock market crash was not the sole reason for their enactment, federal securities law came into place following the Stock Market Crash of 1929 and the resulting Great Depression. Prior to that point, the stock market was very much caveat emptor – buyer beware. There were no regulations on what information an investor was required to be given, nor any limitations on what stock promoters were permitted to tell prospective investors. There was also no control over the buying and selling of securities. The result of these three elements was a wildly speculative market, where unscrupulous stock promoters sold stock in fictitious companies to wealthy and not-so-wealthy investors. Because speculation was so prevalent, prices were being fueled and driven by rumors and greed, pushing the market upward at a dizzying rate. As time passed, however, the fictitious companies failed to produce any earnings, and the truth behind the fiction became clear. The resulting stock market crash was devastating. Many wealthy investors – and not-so-wealthy investors – lost everything. The impact to the United States economy was also drastic and was a major cause of the Great Depression.

The United States government had for some time been seeking a way to establish a regulatory framework over the stock market, as the same factors which were attributed the stock market crash had been occurring for several years. The crash (and resulting financial devastation), however, was the impetus needed for the government to take action. And so the 1933 Act and the 1934 Act were born as a way to regulate the market, ensure that full, complete and accurate disclosure was made by business entities and stock promoters, and that unknowledgeable, modest-income investors, the so-called "widows and orphans," were granted extra protections. The Securities and Exchange Commission was also formed as the regulatory authority to oversee compliance by business entities, stock exchanges and stock promoters. Both Acts are sweeping in scope and are designed to cast the widest net possible over securities-related transactions.

This wide net includes the very term "security." A security is defined under Section 2(1) of the 1933 Act as including stocks, bonds and debentures. However, the 1933 Act also includes investment contracts in its definition of security, and it is into this area that Limited Partnership interests and LLC membership interests may fall.

Under the 1933 Act and the 1934 Act, business entities wishing to sell interests in themselves are required to register those interests with either the state or federal securities commission or both, depending on the offering. The registration process involves preparing a lengthy disclosure document discussing the history of the business entity and its operations, which must, in most cases, be accompanied by audited financial statements. This is an expensive and onerous burden for a business entity, and seems very out of place in a closely held business entity, such as a Family Limited Partnership, which has been designed to transfer wealth from parents to children.

Fortunately, the legislators drafting the 1933 Act and 1934 Act recognized there would be situations where sweeping registration requirements would not apply, and created several classes of exemptions. Business entities meeting one or more of these exemptions are not required to register their securities under the Acts. In addition, in two special circumstances, Family Limited Partnership interests are not even considered to be a security, thus removing them entirely from the requirements of the Acts.

Securities Registration Exemptions for Limited Partnership Interests

The two most common registration exemptions used in the context of Limited Partnerships are Section 4(2) – private placement exemption and Section 3(a)(11) – intrastate exemption of the 1933 Act. These exemptions may be used in the following situations:

> <u>Section 4(2) – Private Placement Exemption</u>. Section 4(2) allows for securities to be exempt from registration where they are not offered to the "public" and no advertising or solicitation is used to attract investors. The court has interpreted this exemption to apply to situations where the parties, for various reasons, are not members of the "public"

and do not need the protection of the 1933 Act. For example, a Family Limited Partnership is not considered to be "public." It is made up of family members who know and trust each other, and there is no need to advertise or conduct any outside search for investors. Where the Limited Partnership is being used as a vehicle to transfer wealth from one generation to another, the younger members are not being required to buy into the Limited Partnership, rather they are being gifted interests. This scenario may be an exempt transaction. However, when an LP is being used as a syndication vehicle for real estate investment or a film deal and numerous investors are required you may need to consider using Regulation D, discussed ahead.

Section 3(a)(11) – Intrastate Offering Exemption. This section of the 1933 Act allows for sales of securities to be exempt from registration where all persons involved are resident within the same state, and the business entity carries on business only within that same state. This can be applied to a Family Limited Partnership situation where the whole family lives within the same state, and the property or other assets that are held by the partnership are also located within that state. Nevertheless, state securities regulations may apply. Be sure to consult your professional advisor on such issues.

SEC Rule 147. Although Section 3(a)(11) of the 1933 Act indicates that all members and assets of a Family Limited Partnership must be resident within the same state, under Rule 147 of the 1933 Act, a registration exemption is offered to Family Limited Partnerships where only 80 percent of the limited partners or assets are located in one state.

When is a Limited Partnership interest not a security?

Limited Partnership interests have been found by the courts to be securities when limited partners who exercise no control of the operations and management of Limited Partnership hold them. This finding was made by applying a two-part test, which asked (i) whether consideration (i.e., money) has changed hands for the interest, and (ii) whether the investment in the Limited Partnership was made with the expectation of receiving a profit through the management efforts of others. Applied to a Limited Partnership interest, it is clear that where an individual transfers assets, cash or property into a Limited Partnership in return for a Limited Partnership interest, consideration has changed hands, meeting the first part of the test. It is also clear that where a general partner manages the Limited Partnership, and the limited partners have no control over the business operations, the limited partners will receive profits through the managerial efforts of another, meeting the second part of the test.

However, there are two instances in which Limited Partnership interests are not considered to be securities, as follows:

Gifted Limited Partnership Interests. The 1933 Act defines the "sale" of a security as a transaction whereby someone disposes of a security for value. Where no value changes hands (*e.g.*, a parent gifts a Limited Partnership interest to a child), the gifted interest is not considered to be a security and is not subject to any registration requirements. However, the gifted Limited Partnership interest is considered to be a security when the child subsequently attempts to transfer or sell the interest.

General Partner Interest. The Limited Partnership interest granted to a general partner, in consideration of his or her role of managing the business affairs of a Limited Partnership, is not considered a security under the 1933 Act. However, the general partner must be in control of the Limited Partnership. Where the Limited Partnership Agreement is drafted in such a way as to limit the general partner's abilities to act, or where a general partner is subordinate to a managing general partner because of his or her inexperience or lack of knowledge of business affairs, then his or her interest will be considered to be a security.

Securities Qualifications for LLC Membership Interests

LLC membership interests are treated in the same fashion as a Limited Partnership interest in many instances. However, because an LLC is also more frequently used as a business entity for non-related individuals and is able to function along many of the same lines as a regulation C Corporation, it is more difficult to escape from the provisions of the 1933 Act and 1934 Act.

Designation as a Security

As with a Limited Partnership interest, an LLC membership interest will be considered to be a security when a member invests in a manager-managed LLC by way of providing cash or transferring assets into the LLC in return for a membership interest, and does not exert any direct control or management over the LLC. Gifting of LLC interests is permitted and is not considered to be a security. LLC membership interests held by the manager(s) will not be considered securities, as long as manager(s) are exerting control over the LLC. However, where there is a team of managers, and not all managers are able to make decisions independently, then the membership interests held by these junior managers will be considered to be securities. When the LLC is member-managed, all members are considered equally responsible for the business and operations of the LLC, and therefore their membership interests are not considered securities.

It is important to remember that each state has its own interpretation of what is and isn't a security. For example, in Alaska, New Mexico, Ohio and Vermont, all membership interests are considered to be securities, no matter what the makeup of the LLC.

Securities Registration Exemptions for Membership Interests

LLCs may also use Section 4(2) of the 1933 Act to sell membership interests to individuals personally known or related to the managers and who have access to information regarding the LLC. No advertising or general solicitations for investments may be made.

However, unlike Family Limited Partnerships, membership interests in an LLC are often held by non-related parties. As the number of members in an LLC increases, so does the remoteness of the relationship to the managers. By the time you're selling membership interests to the 100th member, it is becoming unlikely that this member will be personally known to you. It may also be unlikely that no advertising or solicitation will have been used to attract them. If you are unable to prove a personal or business relationship, the LLC will be disqualified from using the section 4(2) exemption.

The intrastate exemption found under Section 3(a)(11) is also available to LLCs; however, this requires that all LLC members and all LLC assets and business operations be located within the same state. "Business Operations" in this instance means anything relating to your business, from purchasing supplies to forwarding promotional flyers. If you purchase materials or supplies from outside the LLC's home state, have out-of-state customers or even mail advertising flyers out-of-state, the LLC will be ineligible to use this exemption, as well.

So, assuming your Operating Agreement allows you to sell membership interests and your members have approved the sale, how do you raise capital for your LLC and sell membership interests if you don't meet either of these two exemptions? Also, if you are using an LP to syndicate real estate, do a film deal or other project that brings together non-related investors, how do you do the deal within the securities laws?

Regulation D Exemptions

If your LLC or LP is disqualified from issuing securities under either Section 4(2) or 3(a)(11), then the easiest and most common method of selling LLC membership interests or LP partnership interests to outside, non-related individuals is under Rules 504, 505 or 506 of Regulation D of the 1933 Act. Regulation D sets out three circumstances under which unregistered securities may be sold by a business entity. In all cases a disclosure document must be prepared; however, the level of information it needs to contain will vary significantly, depending on the type of investor the LLC or LP is seeking.

Investor Types

There are two types of investors: accredited, and non-accredited. In a nutshell, an accredited investor is someone with over $1 million in assets or a yearly income of $200,000 or more (or, a joint income with spouse of $300,000 per year). Accredited investors are considered by securities authorities to be sophisticated and knowledgeable enough to not need protection. Accredited investors may waive the right to receive a disclosure document. In fact, if you can find accredited investors who are willing to invest in your LLC and waive their right to receive a disclosure document, then you may be able to sell membership interests to them without much more than filing a Form D notice with the Securities and Exchange Commission in Washington and, in some cases, with the investor's home state.

A non-accredited investor is someone who doesn't meet this asset or income test. Selling to non-accredited investors is a completely different story. They must be provided with a full disclosure document, containing a five-year history of the LLC or LP, its business operations, future plans and strategies, and financial information. Selling to non-accredited investors also requires that you provide them with current audited financial statements, which can add significantly to the cost of raising money.

Rule 504 Exemption

Rule 504 provides an exemption from registration for a sale of securities totaling no more than $1 million during any 12-month period, to both accredited and non-accredited investors. However, Rule 504 also allows for advertising and general solicitation of investors. Because of this factor, as well as the inclusion of non-accredited investors, a comprehensive disclosure document containing audited financial statements is required. There is also a requirement that the materials be sent to the Securities and Exchange Commission; however, the filing is not subject to Federal review other than a determination that all of the required elements are contained within the disclosure document (*e.g.*, audited financial statements are attached).

Unfortunately, although Regulation D is a federal regulation, because of the permission of advertising and solicitation of non-accredited investors, some states prohibit a Rule 504 offering outright, and many state securities agencies require that a Rule 504 transaction be registered at the state level. This means that if you are planning on selling membership interests in six states, six different state securities authorities will be reviewing your disclosure materials. You can minimize this impact by selling only to states that have adopted the Uniform Limited Offering Exemption, as your materials may be prepared to one single standard; however, it can still be a time-consuming and costly process. In addition, many states have added extra requirements over and above those found in the Uniform Limited Offering Exemption, including a merit review requirement that allows a state securities authority to not only review your materials to make sure they are in compliance with the disclosure requirements, but also to determine whether your business entity is a suitable investment for a non-accredited investor.

Rule 505 Exemption

Rule 505 allows a business entity to sell up to $5 million worth of securities per offering. There is no advertising or general solicitation permitted under a Rule 505 offering, and non-accredited investor participation is limited to 35 individuals. This has the effect of removing the right of review from individual states, leaving you with just the federal requirements with which to comply. A disclosure document will be required, and, if you intend to sell to non-accredited investors, audited financial statements must be included. A notice, called a Form D, must be filed with the Securities and Exchange Commission within 15 days of the first sale of securities, together with a copy of your disclosure materials. There is no fee to file the Form D.

Sales must also be registered in every state where investors reside. To conduct a registration filing (sometimes referred to as a "blue-sky filing"), you must notify each state of the sale or sales made to investors residing in that state. Notification usually consists of filing a copy of the federal Form D, together with your disclosure materials and a fee within a certain period of time after making a sale in that state.

Rule 506 Exemption

Rule 506 is the most commonly used of the three Regulation D exemptions. As with Rule 505, under Rule 506 no advertising or general solicitation is permitted, and non-accredited investor participation is limited to 35 individuals. There is no right of review by any state, and the amount of money you may raise per offering is unlimited. Also in line with Rule 505, a disclosure document will be required and must contain audited financial statements where non-accredited investors are participating. Again a Form D must be filed with the Securities and Exchange Commission within 15 days of the first sale of securities, together with a copy of your disclosure materials, and you must conduct registration, or "blue-sky" filings in every state into which a security is sold.

In many family-operated, or small, closely-held LLCs and LPs, the securities filing requirements set out above will not apply. As we discussed earlier, Limited Partnerships gifted to children are not considered securities, nor are Limited Partnership or membership interests held by general partners or managers. Subsequent sales or transfers of these interests may well be considered securities though, and it is important that you seek the advice of a qualified securities lawyer before attempting to sell or transfer interests. The penalties for not complying with securities requirements at the state and federal level are severe and can include monetary fines as well as criminal charges, sanctions against future business activities and possible jail time.

There is one other exemption that should be mentioned here: Known as the Rule 4(1)(1/2) exemption, this is an informal and unwritten (but legal) method of conducting an isolated transfer of security from one individual directly to another. The security must have been held for a minimum of two years, and the member or limited cannot have used any form of advertising to secure a purchaser. For example, you cannot put up a general notice on your home Web page telling one and all that you've got an interest in an LLC or LP that you'd like to get rid of. However, assuming that you are able to locate someone or an entity interested in purchasing your interest, the procedure is simply to write to the LLC or LP, advising that you have held the interest for the two-year minimum and would like to transfer it, under Rule 4(1)(1/2). The LLC or LP may require the you to obtain an opinion from legal counsel stating you have met all of the requirements to use this exemption, including holding the interest for the required two-year period, and there is no legal reason why the transfer cannot be conducted. Again though, the best practice is to properly draft the Operating or Partnership Agreement to provide for a transfer/resale mechanism.

Additional Contributions

An issue may arise when members or partners have agreed to contribute additional capital to the entity at a later date. Oral promises to contribute additional monies are not only difficult to enforce but may be prohibited by state statute, as in Missouri. However, many state statutes provide that a written agreement to put more money into the entity is enforceable. Some states even allow for the forfeiture of a member's LLC interest for failure to additionally contribute. Interestingly, certain states specifically prohibit such a forfeiture in a Limited Partnership scenario.

As a practical matter, to enforce additional contributions, the agreement must be in writing. As additional security, the agreement should provide that the member/partner's interest is encumbered (secured) and held by the entity until the full contribution is made. In the event the full amount is not paid, the interest is then defaulted and taken back by the entity.

Frequently Asked Questions

What is the nature of an entity interest?

An LLC or LP interest is the personal property of the member or partner. It may be held in any legal form, such as joint tenancy, separate propertgy or community property. Many people hold such interests in the name of their living trust.

How much capital must be contributed to an LLC/LP?

While the organizers themselves must deal with the issue of adequate capitalization, as a general rule there is no minimum amount that must be contributed. Some states do (or will) require that a reasonable amount be contributed to avoid piercing the limited liability veil for a lack of adequate capitalization.

What is the difference between an LLC/LP interest and an LLC/LP unit?

Both refer to an ownership interest. Technically, the unit of ownership in an LLC or LP, like stock or shares in a Corporation, is an interest. In some cases, units may refer to an aggregate of interests. For example, a PPM may offer one LLC/LP unit, which represents 1,000 interests. An interest, of course, is tied to a percentage ownership of the entity.

If an LLC/LP decides to have a buy-sell agreement should it be a separate document or included in the Operating/Partnership Agreement?

If you want the terms to apply to all existing and future members/partners you may want to include it in the Operating/Partnership Agreement. A separate buy-sell agreement may be useful in situations that did not apply to all interest holders.

Can a member or partner loan money to the entity?

Yes, unless the filing or organizational documents provide otherwise, a member or a partner can lend money to (or guarantee the debts of) the entity. The better practice is to completely disclose the transaction to the other members or partners.

Can a member or partner borrow money from the entity?

Yes, a member or a partner may borrow from the entity unless otherwise prohibited by the filing or organizational documents. The better practice is to provide complete disclosure to all members/partners of such a transaction.

Are the securities laws an issue when I transfer my LLC or LP interest?

Yes, securities laws are an issue during transfers. You must first look to the language in the Operating Agreement or Partnership Agreement to determine the restrictions on the transferability of your interests. Assuming you can proceed to transfer or sell your interests, you must find an applicable exemption before the transfer will be completed. A basic rule of thumb is to make sure you have held your interests for at least two years in order to qualify to use Rule 4(1)(1/2).

Should a general partner receive a Limited Partnership certificate?

While it is not required, the better practice is to issue certificates of ownership to all general and limited partners (and LLC members). The general partner will receive a Limited Partnership certificate reflecting his or her ownership in the Limited Partnership. The general partner will not receive a separate General Partnership certificate.

Can member(s)/partner(s) bring derivative actions on behalf of the LLC/LP?

A derivative action is a legal proceeding started on behalf of an LLC/LP by a member or a partner when a manager or general partner fails to take action on behalf of the entity. If authorized in the Operating/Partnership Agreement, a derivative action can be brought. However, if the agreement is silent, state law will apply, and each state is different. For example, Nevada allows limited partners to bring derivative actions but is silent on LLC members bringing them.

Chapter Six
The Importance of Following the Formalities

One of the selling points of the LLC is its flexibility. People will tell you: "You can do anything with an LLC. You can have one class of members or seven classes of members, four of which are voting, two of which are non-voting and one which represents debt that can convert to equity in ten years, but still gets to vote in every year that an American League team wins the World Series. You can provide for all-expense-paid annual meetings in Fiji or, as in a Limited Partnership, hold no meetings at all and not ever be bothered with any paperwork whatsoever. The flexibility is incredible."

Yes, it is noted that flexibility is a good thing. The nimble and responsive are beating out the slow and formal in all forms of business activity around the world.

However, when flexibility completely supercedes formality, problems can – and will – arise. And the problems are significant.

In the corporate setting, the failure to follow corporate formalities can cause the loss of limited liability protection and result in personal liability for your business's debts and claims. This "piercing of the corporate veil" is a bad thing, and totally defeats the purpose of setting up a limited liability entity in the first place.

In the LLC setting, as we have discussed, a comprehensive body of law has not yet been developed to define the rights and responsibilities of LLC members and managers. However, it is quite easy to foresee that courts will allow an LLC's veil of limited liability to be pierced. In fact, Colorado has already enacted a statute that states:

> "In any case in which a party seeks to hold to the members of a limited liability company personally responsible for the alleged improper actions of the limited liability company, the court shall apply the case law which interprets the conditions and

circumstances under which the corporate veil of a corporation may be pierced under Colorado Law." (Colorado Revised Statutes Annotated, Section 7-80-107(1)).

Another indicator of what may result in terms of piercing the LLC veil comes from Germany. As stated earlier, LLCs were first authorized in Germany in 1892 and are known as Gesellschaft mit beschranker Haftung, or GmbH. (Thank goodness for the universality of abbreviations.) The GmbH is now the most utilized entity for doing business in Germany. With over 100 years of case law, German courts have developed a standard for piercing the GmbH (LLC) veil based on factors including the failure to follow formalities, commingling of assets, and undercapitalization. One can anticipate that American and other common law courts will follow the German courts in allowing the LLC veil to be pierced.

In the Limited Partnership setting, it is noted that many Limited Partnership Agreements provide that their limited partners are only allowed to vote on major issues. Nevertheless, it is still the better practice to hold an annual Limited Partnership meeting, if only to avoid miscommunication and misunderstanding, as well as to provide evidence of business formality. (It should be noted that when the IRS audits a Family Limited Partnership it seeks evidence that meetings have been held.) For all the same reasons, an annual general partners' meeting should be held. This is especially true when, as in most instances, the general partner is a Corporation formed to limit personal liability. The corporate general partner is bound by the corporate law requirement of holding annual directors and stockholders meetings anyway. Where the Corporation exists only to be a corporate general partner, the annual corporate directors meeting can also serve as the annual general partners' meeting, thus saving time and requiring only one set of minutes for both entities.

While not all states require annual meetings of the members or partners, as mentioned above, the better practice is to hold such meetings. When some court someday holds that, despite no state requirement to do so, failure to hold annual meetings is evidence of a lack of LLC/LP business formality, you will want to have a minute book chock full of annual meeting minutes to overcome any such challenge.

And because it is prudent to follow the basic formalities, here are the simple rules:

1. *Annual Filings.* After filing your initial Articles of Organization or an LP-1 Certificate of Limited Partnership, you will need to file an annual report and pay an annual fee to your state. It is not difficult. In Wyoming, for example, the annual report consists of a one-page list of managers or general partners, and the annual fee is $50.
2. *Minutes of Meetings.* As discussed, it is good protection to hold annual meetings and to prepare minutes of these meetings. Our firm charges $150 per year to perform this service. Others may charge less. Or, you can quite easily do it yourself.
3. *Entity Notice.* It is very important that you let the world know that you are operating as an LLC or LP, as opposed to operating as an individual, Sole Proprietorship or other format. On your business cards, letterhead, invoices, company checks, brochures and the like you must identify yourself as doing business as an LLC or LP. Do not just use "J & G Consulting," when you are J & G Consulting, LLC. You want the world to know that you are an LLC or an LP. Likewise, all contracts should be signed by you as the "Manager of J & G Consulting, LLC," or "Corporate General Partner of G & M Properties, LP,," etc. Signing your name without your entity management designation can lead to personal liability.
4. *Separate Bank Account.* You cannot run an entity's banking out of your own personal bank account. An

LLC or an LP is a separate tax entity with its own tax identification number. You must maintain a separate and independent bank account at all times.

5. *Separate Tax Returns.* Because the LLC or LP is a separate tax entity, it is necessary to file a separate entity tax return. Listing revenue and/or expenses on your personal tax return that properly belong on the entity's tax return is not a good idea.
6. *Resident Agent.* You should not use a resident agent that will move without notice or go out of business. The resident agent's job is to accept service of process (a lawsuit) on your behalf. If that firm is out of business it is a reflection on your lack of formality, as it is your duty to make certain that you have a proper resident agent in place. As well, if you do not pay the resident agent's annual service fee so that it withdraws as your representative and you fail to secure the services of another resident agent, it is a very clear sign of a lack of business formality. You must have a paid-up acting resident agent in place.[2]

Failure to follow these six simple rules can allow a creditor to pierce the veil of limited liability and seek personal liability.

So, just how can the veil be pierced?

Case Number 6 - Patrick and Steve

Patrick Faulkner and Steve Turpie grew up together in Grand Junction, Colorado. They both played rugby while attending Colorado College in Colorado Springs and after graduating became business partners. After many months of bartending double-shifts, they scraped together enough money to put a down payment on a fixer-upper duplex. It needed a new roof, some paint and newer fixtures. Patrick and Steve decided to put their own time, energy and sweat into the

---

[2] You may want to visit www.altacian.com for a very cost-effective resident agent plan.

project and, as they projected and hoped, turn the property for a profit and then move on to the next project.

Patrick and Steve decided the best way to both hold the real estate and protect themselves was to form a Limited Liability Company.

In preparation for buying their property, Patrick and Steve filed Articles of Organization with the Colorado Secretary of State. They did not use an attorney or consult with an accountant ahead of time, because as a start-up, Patrick and Steve felt they needed to save money wherever possible. They recalled that an organizational meeting was needed, but kept putting it off, and eventually forgot about holding the meeting altogether.

Patrick and Steve did not know that an LLC, as a separate legal entity, needed to file a Tax ID number (EIN – Employer Identification Number) request with the IRS. If they had gone to a bank to open an LLC bank account they would have learned this, as banks will not open entity accounts without an EIN number for the LLC (or LP, for that matter). Instead, the two just assumed that they could use their own personal bank accounts and sort out what is what later. Monies that Patrick and Steve use to advance the company were paid out of their personal accounts directly to vendors. As things progressed, they tried to keep up by putting the checks they had each written for the property into a designated cupboard in their kitchen.

Six months ago Patrick and Steve received a letter from the Colorado Secretary of State's office requesting the payment of the upcoming year's annual fees. The letter also said they needed to return the check with the List of Managers for the upcoming year. They received a separate letter from their LLC's resident agent, requesting that they pay the upcoming year's resident agent fees. Patrick and Steve did not really understand what was needed, and so both requests wound up being put into the kitchen cupboard.

Patrick recalled hearing that when you received the request from the state it meant that it is time to hold some sort of annual meeting. But, he thought to himself, the LLC was just him and Steve. They spoke every day. What did they possibly have to meet about?

At some point during the year the power company needed a form to be signed to switch service over at the duplex. Steve signed it, writing "Steve Turpie" on the signature line, and sent it back.

Patrick and Steve proceeded with the remodel of the duplex. They worked one bartending shift each and the rest of the time they spent at the duplex, working away. After Patrick and Steve completed remodeling one side of the duplex, they rented it out. But, because they hadn't opened up a bank account in the name of the LLC, the rent check was made payable to Patrick Faulkner.

And then one of the tenants was injured. The roof caved in on her, resulting in serious medical problems. While Steve and Patrick had some insurance, their insurance company asserted that they were grossly negligent in their construction methods and denied coverage. Shortly thereafter, Patrick and Steve learned what it meant to "pierce the LLC veil."

In Colorado, by statute, the veil of limited liability as to individual members of an LLC can be pierced, or set aside, in cases where the members fail to follow certain formalities. Where Members conduct their business as though the LLC does not exist, or are so careless in their dealings that proper recognition of a separate entity is ignored, personal liability to each member may attach.

A piercing of the veil of limited liability can be devastating, as it was for Steve and Patrick. The tenant's attorney had absolutely no problem proving a complete lack of entity formality. The evidence was:

- The LLC Charter has been revoked for failure to file Annual Reports
- No organization or annual meetings of the members or managers were ever held
- An EIN was never obtained for the entity from the IRS
- No LLC bank account was ever opened

- Rent payments were made to Patrick, not the LLC
- No LLC tax returns were ever filed
- The resident agent had withdrawn and was not replaced
- In at least one contract, Steve had signed as an individual, and not as a Manager of the LLC

Patrick and Steve were each held personally liable for the tenant's injuries. All of their work, efforts and dreams were lost for the failure to take some very simple protective steps.

To prevent the veil of limited liability of your LLC (or LP) from ever being pierced, you need to develop a mind-set of separateness. You are not the entity. The entity is not you. You will help the entity by serving as a manager or general partner and holding an interest in it. In return, the LLC or LP will help you with limited liability and other protections. This mutually beneficial relationship cannot last if separateness is not respected.

To maintain separateness, consider the following rules as guidance:

1. Never see the entity's assets as your own. They are not. They belong to the LLC or LP. Title is (or should be) held in the entity's name and you as a manager or partner have a duty to administer those assets in the best interests of all of the members and partners. The fact that you own 10 percent, 50 percent or 100 percent of the entity is of no consequence. You only own an interest in the LLC/LP, not in the asset itself. You are one step removed from ownership of the assets.
2. Never start out undercapitalized. In some states, including California, failure to properly capitalize the entity can lead to a piercing of the veil of limited liability. If it is going to cost $75,000 to open your business, do not start signing contracts and making obligations with vendors with only $2,000 in the bank.
3. Never commingle entity and personal assets or monies. Deposit all entity monies into the entity's separate account. Putting LLC or LP money into your personal account and later paying the entity back is a bad idea.

Using the entity's money to cover a personal obligation, even though you pay it back, is another bad idea.

4. Never divert entity funds to non-business uses. Protestations of honest mistakes are useless. You have a duty to know what is right and wrong. If you have the slightest suspicion or twinge of guilt, do not do it. It is not worth the trouble, and it is not worth the consequences.
5. Never sell interests in the LLC or LP without formal approval of the Managers or General Partners. To do otherwise is a securities violation.
6. Never go a year without holding an annual meeting. Even though your state law may not require it, as discussed, you will be much better off legally, as well as politically with your investors/partners, if you hold and memorialize meetings. Minutes of annual meetings – documents proving that you understand the difference between you and the entity on a continuing basis – are a prudent must.

The annual and consistent preparation of meeting minutes is worthy of greater discussion.

Minutes of Meetings

An excellent way to prevent having your veil of limited liability pierced is to prove your formality by preparing and keeping minutes of your manager/member or general partner/limited partner meetings.

People frequently state how difficult it is to prepare annual meeting minutes. But when it comes down to losing your personal assets versus an hour of typing, well, there is just no comparison.

The following are samples of minutes for an LLC and an LP. There are minutes for the first organizational meeting, and minutes for the subsequent annual meetings of manager/members and general partners/limited partners. Also note that, since many general partners are Corporations, which are required to hold annual director and stockholder meetings anyway, you may use corporate minutes for the general partner meeting. Corporate minutes are found in my book, *Own Your Own Corporation.* Please note that the minutes contained herein are generic and may not fit your specific situation. Be sure to consult with your advisors as to their applicability. Also note that many of these forms are available on the CD-ROM that accompanies the *Use Your Own Corporation* (Altacian, 2003) product.

If this still seems too difficult to bother with, do not worry. Our associate, Altacian Corporate Services, or another service provider can do it for you. Altacian's fee is $150 per year. Other service providers may be more or less. The important thing is that the minutes are prepared, either by you or by someone else, on an annual basis to preserve your entity's limited liability protection.

MINUTES OF THE FIRST MEETING OF THE MEMBERS OF XYZ, LLC

The first meeting of Members of XYZ, LLC (the "LLC") was held on ______________________, 200___. The meeting was called to order by Jack Smith, a Manager of the LLC, and the following Members, being a majority of the Members of the LLC and representing the Membership Interests as indicated, were present:

Jack Smith, representing ______ Membership Interests
Jill Jones, representing ______ Membership Interests
Maria Perez, representing ______ Membership Interests
Otto Schultz, representing ______ Membership Interests

Maria Perez acted as Secretary of the Meeting.

The Chairman reviewed the Articles of Organization that had been filed with the Secretary of State of the State of [STATE OF ORGANIZATION] and directed the Secretary to insert a certified copy of the Articles of Organization in the minute books as part of these minutes.

The Chairman then presented the Members with a draft form of Operating Agreement, which provided the following significant terms:

1. One or more Managers shall be elected by the Members on a yearly basis at each Annual Member Meeting. Members shall have the right to remove a Manager at any time without cause by a [unanimous OR simple majority OR two-thirds majority] vote of the Members.
2. Amendments to the Operating Agreement must be approved by a [unanimous OR simple majority OR two-thirds majority] vote of the Members.
3. The Manager or Managers shall have complete and exclusive control over the management and day-to-day business and affairs of the LLC. Any disagreements between Managers as to actions of the LLC must be put to a vote of the Members and a [unanimous OR simple majority OR two-thirds majority] vote is required to proceed. The Members shall have no rights to participate in the management or control of the business and affairs of the Company, and shall have only the voting rights specifically set forth in the Operating Agreement.

4. Notwithstanding the above, the Manager or Managers require a [unanimous OR simple majority OR two-thirds majority] vote of the Members in order to:
    - Do any act in contravention of this Agreement, as amended from time to time;
    - Do any act which would make it impossible to carry on the ordinary business of the Company, provided that actions of the Managers in accordance with the purposes of the Company or rights and powers granted under this Agreement shall not be considered to breach this clause;
    - Confess any judgment or settle any claims asserted against the Company;
    - Possess Company property, or assign rights in any Company property, for other than a Company purpose;
    - Knowingly perform any act that would subject any Member to liability as a General Partner of a partnership in any jurisdiction;
    - Commingle funds of the Company with funds of any other person;
    - Lend to any person any of the cash funds or other Company property;
    - Purchase or lease Company property from the Company or sell or lease property to the Company;
    - Guarantee the indebtedness of any person or cause, suffer or permit any Company property to secure or become collateral for any indebtedness of any person other than the Company;
    - Amend the number of Manager(s) set forth in the Operating Agreement;
    - Unless such Manager or Managers have been appointed as the Tax Matters Member for the Company, extend the statute of limitations for assessment of tax deficiencies against the Company and/or its Members with respect to adjustments to the Company's federal, state or local tax returns;
    - Unless such Manager or Managers have been appointed as the Tax Matters Member for the Company, as provided herein, represent the Company, the Members or Interest Holders before taxing authorities or courts of competent jurisdiction in tax matters affecting the Company, the Members and any Interest Holders in their capacities as such, or to execute any agreement or other documents relating to or affecting tax matters, including agreement or other documents that bind the Members and Interest

Holders with respect to tax matters or otherwise affect the rights of the Company, Members and Interest Holders;

- Prosecute or defend claims by or against the Company or affecting title to Company property, and, unless such Manager or Managers have been appointed as the Tax Matters Member for the company, to contest any determination by the Internal Revenue Service or any state or local taxing authority as to any matters affecting the Company, any Members or Interest Holders;

Following a review and discussion of the Operating Agreement, the Chairman called for a vote by the Members, and:

> **UPON MOTION**, duly made, seconded and carried, IT WAS RESOLVED THAT the Operating Agreement in the form attached to these Minutes be and is hereby approved, and that the Operating Agreement shall be circulated among all the Members for signature and entry into the Minute Book.

There being no further business to come before the meeting, UPON MOTION duly made, seconded and unanimously carried, the meeting was adjourned.

____
Secretary

CONSENT RESOLUTIONS OF THE FIRST MEETING OF THE MANAGER(S) OF XYZ, LLC

I/We, the undersigned, being the sole/all of the Manager(s) of the LLC, do hereby waive notice of the time, place and purpose of the First Meeting of the Managers of the LLC and DO HEREBY CONSENT to the adoption of the following resolutions:

RESOLVED THAT the form of Membership Interest Certificate submitted to this meeting is adopted and approved as the Membership Interest Certificate of the LLC, and that a copy of the Membership Interest Certificate shall be inserted into the minute book.

RESOLVED FURTHER, that Membership Interests Certificates be issued to the following Members, representing the interests set out as follows:

Cert No.	Name	Number of Membership Interests
1	Jack Smith	____________
2	Jill Jones	____________
3	Maria Perez	____________
4	Otto Schultz	____________

RESOLVED THAT the salary of the Manager shall be determined at a later date.

RESOLVED THAT the Manager of the LLC be authorized and directed to pay all charges and expenses incident to the formation and organization of the LLC and to reimburse all persons who have made any disbursements for such charges and expenses.

RESOLVED THAT the LLC shall reimburse each Manager and authorized Member for any reasonable necessary expenses that they incur in connection with the purposes of the LLC and in furtherance of its business.

RESOLVED FURTHER, that it shall be the policy of this LLC to reimburse each Manager or authorized Member, or to pay directly on behalf of each Manager or authorized Member, necessary and ordinary out-of-pocket expenses incidental to travel for all business activities of the LLC requiring travel.

RESOLVED THAT beginning with the month in which the LLC begins business, the LLC commence amortizing its organizational expense over a period of sixty (60) months in accordance with Section 248 of the Internal Revenue Code.

RESOLVED THAT [NAME OF BANK OR OTHER FINANCIAL INSTITUTION] is designated as the depository for the general account of the LLC, and all checks, drafts and orders on any of the accounts with the depository may be signed by the following: [NAME OF INDIVIDUALS ABLE TO SIGN CHECKS, I.E., JACK SMITH and JILL JONES] in their capacity as Manager(s) of the LLC. The Manager is authorized and directed to execute any documents necessary to open and continue any accounts with the depository.

RESOLVED FURTHER that a copy of such documents be inserted into the Minute Book of the LLC.

RESOLVED THAT [NAME OF RESIDENT AGENT APPOINTED WHEN ARTICLES FILED], be, and hereby is appointed Registered Agent for the LLC in the State of [STATE OF ORGANIZATION]. The office of the Registered Agent is to be located at [ADDRESS OF REGISTERED AGENT].

Optional

RESOLVED FURTHER, that [NAME OF LEGAL COUNSEL, IF ANY] be retained as the Corporation's legal counsel.

RESOLVED THAT Membership Interests shall be issued pursuant to Section 1244 of the Internal Revenue Code. The LLC is authorized to issue Membership Interests in accordance with the provisions of the Operating Agreement, and said Membership Interests shall be issued only for money and other property (other than stock or securities). The Manager or Managers of the LLC are authorized, empowered and directed to perform any and all acts necessary to carry out this plan and to qualify the Membership Interests issued under it as Section 1244 stock as that term is defined in Section 1244 of the Internal Revenue Code and the Regulations thereunder.

RESOLVED THAT ____________________ shall be selected as the fiscal year-end date for the Corporation by filing of a tax return, other appropriate tax form or by any other proper action.

RESOLVED THAT the meetings of the Manager(s) or the Members of the LLC shall be held at the principal office of the LLC or at such other location as the Managers may determine, from time to time, as may be called by the Manager, and that no further notice of such regular meetings need be given.

DATED: ______________________, 200____.

____
Jack Jones, Manager

____
______________________________, Manager

(when you have more than one Manager, add this section)

CERTIFICATION BY SECRETARY

I, ___________________, Acting Secretary for the First Managers Meeting of the LLC, HEREBY CERTIFY that the above-noted Managers represent a quorum of Managers, as is required to conduct business under the Operating Agreement of the LLC.

Dated: ______________________, 200__.

____
______________________________, Secretary

CONSENT RESOLUTIONS OF THE ANNUAL MEETING OF THE MANAGER(S) OF XYZ, LLC (THE "LLC")

I/We, the undersigned, being the sole/all of the Manager(s) of the LLC, do hereby waive notice of the time, place and purpose of the Annual Meeting of the Managers of the LLC and DO HEREBY CONSENT to the adoption of the following resolutions:

> **RESOLVED** that the actions taken in the preceding year on behalf of the LLC, as set out below, be approved and ratified.
>
> - [SET OUT SIGNIFICANT BUSINESS ACTIVITIES HERE, SUCH AS MAJOR CONTRACTS ENTERED INTO, OPENING/CLOSING OF BANK ACCOUNTS, DEBT INCURRED, DEBT OWED TO THE LLC, MOVING OF PREMISES, ETC, ADMISSION OF NEW MEMBERS, TRANSFER OF MEMBERSHIP INTERESTS, ETC.]
>
> **RESOLVED** that the Manager(s) call a Meeting of the Members of the LLC to be held immediately following the conclusion of this Meeting, and present the Members with a report on all business activities conducted by the Manager(s) on behalf of the LLC during the preceding year.

DATED: ______________________, 200____.

____
Jack Jones, Manager
____
______________________________, Manager

(when you have more than one Manager, add this section)

CERTIFICATION BY SECRETARY

I, ___________________, Acting Secretary for the Annual Managers Meeting of the LLC, HEREBY CERTIFY that the above-noted Managers represent a quorum of Managers, as is required to conduct business under the Operating Agreement of the LLC.

Dated: ____________________, 200__.

____
______________________________, Secretary

CONSENT RESOLUTIONS OF ANNUAL MEETING OF MEMBERS OF XYZ, LLC (THE "LLC")

We, the undersigned, being all of the Members (or a majority of the Members) of the above-captioned LLC, do hereby waive notice of the time, place and purpose of the Annual Meeting of the Members of the LLC and DO HEREBY CONSENT to the adoption of the following resolutions:

> **RESOLVED THAT** the following persons or corporate entities are elected as Managers of the LLC for the forthcoming year:
>
> **Jack Jones**
>
> **RESOLVED THAT** the Members approve, confirm and ratify the actions of the Manager for the previous year.

Dated: ___________________________, 200___

____________________________	____________________________
Jack Smith representing ______ Membership Interests	Jill Jones, representing ______ Membership Interests
____________________________	____________________________
Maria Perez, representing ______ Membership Interests	Otto Schultz, representing ______ Membership Interests

CERTIFICATION BY SECRETARY

I, Maria Perez, Secretary at the Annual Meeting of the Members of XYZ, LLC, **HEREBY CERTIFY** that the above-noted Members hold an aggregate total of ________ Membership Interests, representing ________% of the LLC's issued Membership Interests, and that this percentage meets the Member majority required to transact business as set out in the Operating Agreement of the LLC.

Dated: _______________________, 200__.

____
Maria Perez, Secretary

MINUTES OF THE FIRST MEETING OF THE LIMITED PARTNERS OF XYZ, LIMITED PARTNERSHIP

The first meeting of the Limited Partners of XYZ, Limited Partnership (the "LP") was held on ______________________, 200___. The meeting was called to order by Jack Smith, the President and a director of Overlord, Inc., General Partner of the LP and the following Limited Partners, being a majority of the Limited Partners of the LP and representing the Limited Partnership Interests as indicated were present:

Overlord, Inc., representing 2 General Partnership Interests;
Jack Smith, representing 30 Limited Partnership Interests
Jill Jones, representing 30 Limited Partnership Interests
Maria Perez, representing 20 Limited Partnership Interests
Otto Schultz, representing 18 Limited Partnership Interests

Maria Perez acted as Secretary of the Meeting.

The Chairman reviewed the Certificate of Limited Partnership that had been filed with the Secretary of State of the State of [STATE OF ORGANIZATION] and directed the Secretary to insert a certified copy of the Certificate of Limited Partnership in the minute books as part of these minutes.

The Chairman then presented the Limited Partners with a draft form of Limited Partnership Agreement, which provided the following significant terms:

1. The Limited Partnership shall be managed by a General Partner, who shall be accredited a two percent Limited Partnership Interest in consideration for his or her services.
2. The General Partner may only resign or be removed by the Limited Partners in accordance with the Limited Partnership Agreement.
3. The Limited Partners shall have no role in the management of the Limited Partnership except as specifically provided for in the Limited Partnership Agreement.
4. The Limited Partners shall have no voting rights with respect to the Limited Partnership except as specifically provided for in the Limited Partnership Agreement.
5. Transfer of Limited Partnership Interests shall be restricted and only allowed as specifically provided for in the Limited Partnership Agreement.

6. Amendments to the Limited Partnership Agreement may only be made as specifically provided for in the Limited Partnership Agreement.

Following a review and discussion of the Limited Partnership Agreement, the Chairman called for a vote by the Limited Partners, and:

> **UPON MOTION** duly made, seconded and carried, **IT WAS RESOLVED THAT** the Limited Partnership Agreement in the form attached to these Minutes be and is hereby approved, and that the Limited Partnership Agreement shall be circulated among all the General and Limited Partners for signature and entry into the Minute Book.

There being no further business to come before the meeting, **UPON MOTION** duly made, seconded and unanimously carried, it was adjourned.

____
Secretary

CONSENT RESOLUTIONS OF THE FIRST MEETING OF THE GENERAL PARTNER OF XYZ, LIMITED PARTNERSHIP (the "LP")

I, the undersigned, being the General Partner of the LP, HEREBY WAIVE notice of the time, place and purpose of the First Meeting of the General Partner of the LP and HEREBY CONSENT to the adoption of the following resolutions:

RESOLVED THAT the form of Limited Partnership Interest Certificate submitted to this meeting is adopted and approved as the Limited Partnership Interest Certificate of the LP, and a copy of the Limited Partnership Interest Certificate shall be inserted into the minute book.

RESOLVED FURTHER that the Limited Partnership Interests Certificates be issued to the following Members as follows:

Cert No.	*Name*	*Number of Membership Interests*
1	Overlord, Inc.	2 General Partnership Interests
2	Jack Smith	30 Limited Partnership Interests
3	Jill Jones	30 Limited Partnership Interests
4	Maria Perez	20 Limited Partnership Interests
5	Otto Schultz	18 Limited Partnership Interests

RESOLVED THAT additional compensation for the General Partner shall be determined at a later date.

RESOLVED THAT the General Partner of the LP be authorized and directed to pay all charges and expenses incident to the formation and organization of the LP and to reimburse all persons who have made any disbursements for such charges and expenses.

RESOLVED THAT the LP shall reimburse the General Partner for any reasonable necessary expenses they incur in connection with the purposes of the LP and in furtherance of its business.

RESOLVED FURTHER that it shall be the policy of this LP to reimburse the General Partner, or to pay directly on behalf of the General Partner, necessary and ordinary out-of-pocket expenses incidental to travel for all business activities of the LP requiring travel.

RESOLVED THAT beginning with the month in which the LP begins business, the LP commence amortizing its organizational expense over a period of sixty (60) months in accordance with Section 248 of the Internal Revenue Code.

RESOLVED THAT [NAME OF BANK OR OTHER FINANCIAL INSTITUTION] is designated as the depository for the general account of the LP, and all checks, drafts and orders on any of the accounts with the depository may be signed by the following: **Any two Officers and/or Directors of Overlord, Inc.,** in their capacity as General Partners of the LP. The General Partners are authorized and directed to execute any documents necessary to open and continue any accounts with the depository.

RESOLVED FURTHER that a copy of such documents be inserted into the Minute Book.

RESOLVED THAT [NAME OF RESIDENT AGENT APPOINTED WHEN ARTICLES FILED], be, and hereby is appointed Resident Agent for the LP in the State of [STATE OF ORGANIZATION]. The office of the Resident Agent is to be located at [ADDRESS OF RESIDENT AGENT].

Optional

RESOLVED FURTHER, that [NAME OF LEGAL COUNSEL, IF ANY] be retained as the LP's legal counsel.

RESOLVED THAT Limited Partnership Interests shall be issued pursuant to Section 1244 of the Internal Revenue Code. The LP is authorized to issue Limited Partnership Interests in accordance with the provisions of the Limited Partnership Agreement, and said Limited Partnership Interests shall be issued only for money and other property (other than stock or securities). The General Partner is authorized, empowered and directed to perform any and all acts necessary to carry out this plan and to qualify the Limited Partnership Interests issued under it as Section 1244 stock as that term is defined in Section 1244 of the Internal Revenue Code and the Regulations thereunder.

RESOLVED THAT _____________________ shall be selected as the fiscal year-end date for the LP by filing of a tax return, other appropriate tax form or by any other proper action.

RESOLVED THAT the meetings of the General and Limited Partners of the LP shall be held at the principal office of the LP or at such other location as the General Partner may determine, from time to time, as may be called by the General Partner, and that no further notice of such regular meetings need be given.

____

Jack Smith, President, Overlord, Inc.
General Partner of XYZ Limited Partnership

(Use when Corporation is the General Partner of the LP)

CONSENT RESOLUTIONS OF ANNUAL MEETING OF THE DIRECTORS OF OVERLORD, INC. (THE "CORPORATION")

We, the undersigned, being all or a quorum of the Directors of the Corporation, do hereby waive notice of the time, place and purpose of the Annual Meeting of the Directors of the Corporation and DO HEREBY CONSENT to the adoption of the following resolutions:

> **RESOLVED THAT** the following individuals be appointed as Officers of the Corporation, to serve until their resignation or the next Annual Directors Meeting, as evidenced by their signature(s) below:

Name	*Office*
Jack Smith	President
Jill Jones	Secretary
Maria Perez	Treasurer

> **RESOLVED THAT** the actions taken in the preceding year on behalf of the Corporation, on its own behalf and in its capacity as the General Partner of XYZ, Limited Partnership, as set out below, be approved and ratified.
>
> - [SET OUT SIGNIFICANT BUSINESS ACTIVITIES HERE, SUCH AS MAJOR CONTRACTS ENTERED INTO, OPENING/CLOSING OF BANK ACCOUNTS, DEBT INCURRED, DEBT OWED TO THE LLP, MOVING OF PREMISES, ETC, TRANSFER OR CHANGES TO LIMITED PARTNERSHIP INTERESTS, ETC.]
>
> **RESOLVED THAT** the Corporation call a Meeting of the Limited Partners of XYZ, Limited Partnership to be held immediately following the conclusion of this Meeting, and present the Limited Partners with a report on all business activities conducted by the General Partner on behalf of XYZ, Limited Partnership during the preceding year.

DATED: ______________________, 200____.

____
Director

____

Director

CERTIFICATION BY SECRETARY

I, Jill Jones, the Secretary of the Corporation certify that the above-noted Directors represent a quorum of Directors, as is required to conduct business under the Bylaws of the Corporation.

Dated: ______________________, 200__.

____
Jill Jones, Secretary

CONSENT RESOLUTIONS OF ANNUAL MEETING OF THE LIMITED PARTNERS OF XYZ, LIMITED PARTNERSHIP

We, the undersigned, being all the Limited Partners (or a majority of the Limited Partners) of the above-captioned Limited Partnership, do hereby waive notice of the time, place and purpose of the Annual Meeting of the Limited Partners:

The Annual Meeting was chaired by Jack Jones, the President and a Director of Overlord, Inc., the Limited Partnership's General Partner.

Mr. Jones presented a report to the Limited Partners on the business proceedings for the Limited Partnership during the preceding year. In particular, he advised the meeting of the following significant events:

- [SET OUT INDIVIDUAL EVENTS HERE]

Mr. Jones then opened the floor for questions about the preceding year and future years of operation by the Limited Partnership.

Following the conclusion of the question period, the Meeting was adjourned.

Dated: ________________________, 200___

______________________________ Jack Smith representing ______ Limited Partnership Interests	______________________________ Jill Jones representing ______ Limited Partnership Interests
______________________________ Maria Perez representing ______ Limited Partnership Interests	______________________________ Otto Schultz representing ______ Limited Partnership Interests

That was all pretty easy. Especially when compared to losing your home, your car and your bank account. Prepare the Minutes. Follow the formalities.

Frequently Asked Questions

Assuming I prepare annual minutes, where do I keep them?

It is important to keep your minutes in a safe place. Obviously, losing or misplacing them does not fit into your protection strategy. Minute books are sometimes best used for keeping such documents.

What is a minute book?

A minute book is a binder used for holding your meeting minutes as well as Articles of Organization, LP-1 Certificate of Limited Partnership, Certificate of Acceptance of Resident Agent, Operating Agreement, LP Agreement, Membership or LP Interest Certificates and other corporate documents. They generally cost about $80, can be purchased from most good quality stationers or from your formation provider, and, if they force you to be organized, will be money well spent.

What should I include in the minutes?

The following list contains some of the items to be reviewed by the managers, members, general and limited partners, and reflected in the minutes:

- Electing or removing managers or general partners
- Amending the Operating Agreement or LP Agreement
- Approving the issuance of additional membership or LP interests
- Approve the sale of membership interests, or admittance of new members or limited partners
- Declaring dividends or losses

- Entering into major agreements with other parties, including agreements to purchase the LLC or LP
- Entering into employment contracts with key employees
- Approving contracts, leases and other obligations
- Borrowing significant sums of money and the granting of security over assets of the LLC or LP in connection therewith
- Acquiring other businesses or major assets
- Converting LLCs or LPs into a Corporation

Chapter Seven
Asset Protection

LLCs and LPs are frequently used for their asset protection benefits. As every reader knows, there are predators in our society poised to attack for the slightest real or imagined infraction. There are professional plaintiffs who look for ways to get injured on an unsuspecting owner's property. There are gangs in major cities who create car accidents in order to obtain insurance settlements and judgments against law-abiding citizens. And, even more unfortunately, there are attorneys who use the system to gain advantage over high net-worth individuals in a variety of legalistic ways.

The key nowadays is to protect you and your family from wrongful creditor attacks. By holding your assets in an LP or LLC you gain significant asset protection benefits, as discussed in our next case.

As well, an important asset protection strategy is to keep a low profile. By using nominee officers, directors, managers and general partners you may initially defer a potential plaintiff from even defining you as a high net-worth individual. If a name search on the Internet shows you to be president, manager or general partner of one or more entities, and a further search indicates that these entities have value, you are exposed. Instead, by using nominees – persons other than yourself – to be publicly listed as manager, general partner or the like, your name is kept off the public record and the Internet, to your low profile advantage.

You may want to consider using a nominee for some or all of your entities. Our affiliate charges $650 per year for the service. Others may charge more or less. A nominee, by keeping your ownership and involvement confidential, is the first line of defense.

The second line of defense is the charging order.

The charging order procedure is a unique asset protection feature of Limited Partnerships and Limited Liability Companies. In most states, a judgment creditor – an individual or entity who has sued and obtained a court judgment entitling them to damages – may only obtain a charging order against an LP or LLC. This means that a creditor does not get title to the property owned by the LP or LLC but instead only the right to receive the member or partner's distribution.

If a member or partner is allocated profits by an entity in a taxable year but no money flows through to pay the taxes, the result is phantom income. The receipt of tax obligation from an entity without money to at least pay the taxes is a sure way to anger members and partners. Creditors standing in their shoes like it even less.

Here is a quick example of phantom income: Feeney Fisher, LLC has a year-end profit of $100,000. The manager decides to keep all the profits in the LLC for next year's expansion plans. Each of the five 20 percent members receives a K-1 indicating a gain of $20,000 but receive no money from Feeney Fisher, LLC. As such, each member must come out of pocket to pay the taxes. For those in a 35 percent tax bracket they must pay $7,000 for the privilege of being a part of Feeney Fisher, LLC. As managers and general partners have learned: (1) members and partners really do not appreciate phantom income, and (2) it is usually wise to flow through enough money to at least cover the taxes.

Nevertheless, the beauty of phantom income is that creditors are even more frustrated by it. Pursuant to the charging order procedure they get to receive the distributions a member or partner would ordinarily receive – a tax bill of $20,000 with no money for taxes. As a result, the creditor must pay out $7,000 for the privilege of trying to collect on a debt. Many, if not all, creditors consider this good money after bad. And while some practitioners argue that the creditor is not technically required to pay the tax, all agree that the threat of phantom income is useful and an inducement towards settlement.

An example helps explain the concept. Please note that we will use an LP for our case, but that an LLC would apply as well.

Case Number 7 – Cammie and Peter

Cammie and Peter have a profitable bakery distribution business. They started by selling muffins, scones and the like to offices downtown and have grown the business over the years to include distribution to restaurants and convenience stores. After nearly nine years of operating as general partners with full exposure to all risk, their accountant insists it is now time to protect their assets. The urgency is even greater since Cammie and Peter are considering an investment in a much riskier venture – a restaurant. Peter likes the idea of using a Limited Partnership. As was discussed at the beginning of this book, Limited Partnerships are not the most common entities for use with operating businesses (as opposed to holding assets). But for Peter there are overriding reasons to use a Limited Partnership. He wants to maintain control as general partner and yet gift Limited Partnership interests to his and Cammie's twin children.

Cammie and Peter learn from their accountant that they do not want the liability as a general partner of a Limited Partnership. So C & P Management, Inc is formed to be the general partner of C & P Muffins, LP. C & P Management, Inc. has a four percent interest in the Limited Partnership. Because Cammie and Peter may get sued in the new restaurant venture, they can not be the majority owner of C & P Management, Inc. If they are a majority owner, a creditor can get at their shares, assert control over C & P Management, Inc. and, as general partner of C & P Muffins, LP, thwart the whole plan by making distributions from the LP as the creditor sees fit to satisfy his or her debt (in addition, although not applicable in this case, it is best that one spouse not give the other spouse control of the corporate general partner since he or she may be found jointly liable for any debts if the other spouse is sued.) So Cammie and Peter give 60 percent of C & P Management, Inc. to their trusted adult son Tristan. Peter and Cammie are still the chairman, CEO, president, and all other officers of C & P Management, Inc. They have overall authority for both C & P Management, Inc. and, as corporate general partner, over C & P Muffins, LP.

Once the bakery business is contributed to C & P Muffins, LP, they begin a gifting program of Limited Partnership interests. After two years, Peter, Cammie, their son Tristan and their daughter Petra each own Limited Partnership interests of 24 percent of C & P Muffins, LP. The remaining four percent is held by the general partner, C & P Management, Inc. All is in place.

Cammie and Peter have always wanted to own a restaurant. They run into another couple, Lori and Dan, who have food service management experience, and who also want to start a restaurant. Their other friends remind them how risky it is to run a restaurant in their town. It is tough business. Most only last two or three years. But Cammie and Peter and Lori and Dan are confident. They have obtained a five-year lease on the best location in town – right next to City Hall and the Courthouse. The street is well traveled and highly visible. An upscale bistro for the professionals and drivers in the area seems a natural. They are ready to go.

Their accountant suggests they use an S Corporation for the business. Each couple puts up $50,000. Peter loans $25,000 to Dan to complete his contribution. They form Roxy Bistro, Inc., to operate the restaurant. They then obtain a bank loan of $300,000 to complete building improvements. This loan is personally guaranteed by Cammie, Peter, Lori and Dan.

Three weeks after the bistro opens a major announcement is made. The city is to begin construction immediately on a new subway system. The key transfer point is to be downtown next to City Hall. The roads in the two-block area will be closed for several years to accommodate the digging and construction. Cammie and Peter are devastated. No one will be able to get to the restaurant.

Sure enough, in another month, when the roads are closed, the bistro's business drops off significantly. They have no choice but to close the business.

The bank is owed money. Roxy Bistro, Inc., has no assets. But the bank obtained personal guarantees. Being the most solvent of the restaurant's owners, the bank immediately proceeds against Cammie and Peter. Their only personal assets are their respective 24 percent Limited Partnership ownership interests in C & P Muffin, LP.

The bank's exclusive recourse was to obtain a charging order against Peter and Cammie's interest, which means they can not just march into C & P Muffins, LP and take 48 percent of the equipment, furniture and receivables. They have to wait until the corporate general partner decides, in its sole discretion, to make a distribution to the limited partners. The bank gets to stand in Cammie and Peter's shoes and receive whatever is distributed.

While the bank can hope to receive something upon a dissolution of the entity, they have no power to force such an event. If Cammie, Peter and the others decide to continue the business they may outlast the creditor's judgment, which typically must be renewed every, for example, seven years, and in many states expires after a fixed number of years.

Now remember, Cammie and Peter are only president and CEO of C & P Management, Inc. They do not own a majority of the shares because the bank, as creditor, could get a hold of the shares, vote themselves into control of C & P Management and decide, as corporate general partner, to make favorable distributions to C & P Muffins, LP. With their charging order the bank would receive Cammie's 24 percent of those distributions and Peter's 24 percent of distributions.

But as CEO of C & P Management, Inc. without fear of being voted out, thanks to Tristan's ownership, Peter can decide to not make any distributions. So the bank, as well as his other children, gets nothing. And because profits are required to flow through a partnership, Peter can allocate profits on a Form K-1 filing with the IRS but not provide any money to pay the taxes on the gain. Again, this is phantom income and is frustrating for creditors.

Say each 24 percent limited partner receives a taxable gain of $100,000, and the taxes on such a gain are $20,000. Peter decides to hire each of his boys in the business and pays them enough in salary to cover their tax obligation. The only one without money to pay the taxes is the bank. Oh sure, it can pay the taxes – it's a bank. But for the privilege of trying to collect from Peter and Cammie it is going to cost them $20,000 this year. And maybe $40,000 next year. And after the money flows out without any hope of coming in, the bank is ready to settle their claim for 10¢ (or less) on the dollar.

And that is what happens. Cammie and Peter settle the bank's claim for $100,000 and never open a restaurant again.

While each state is different, there are a number of procedural hoops that a judgment creditor must jump through to collect on a charging order. Some include:

- Litigating the case and securing a judgment against a limited partner or member
- Going back to court to obtain a charging order
- Applying to foreclose on the partner/member's interest
- Appointing a receiver to receive any interest holder distributions

As discussed, the steps that a creditor must take to satisfy their debt provide a very large incentive for settlement.

Some readers may question whether the charging order is really fair to the bank. They loaned the money, they have a judgment and they should be able to collect. There are three issues that arise in a discussion of this question:

1. The California Court of Appeals in similar fact situations agreed that the creditor should collect. See Crocker National Bank v. Perroton, 208 Cal. App.3d 1 (1989) and Hellman v. Anderson, 233 Cal. App.3d 840 (1991). The court noted that the original purpose of the

charging order was to protect limited partners who were not debtors and to prevent the interruption of partnership business. They noted its intent was not to allow partners to avoid debts. As remedies, the court in one case ordered the partnership interest sold with the other partners' consent. In the second, where it was found the sale would not interrupt the partnership business, the sale was ordered without the other partners' consent.

This remedy is limited to California at this writing but could be adopted by other states in the future. While it is important to know and recognize this possibility, as discussed below in point three, it should not deter you from using an LP or LLC.

2. In the case above, the bank conducted (or should have conducted) a due diligence investigation into Cammie and Peter's financial condition. As long as the two did not lie on their loan application the bank should have known that their sole assets were Limited Partnership interests that would be difficult to get at. If the bank had a problem with it the solution was simple: do not lend Cammie and Peter the money.
3. The advantage of the charging order is not that it hurts legitimate creditors but that it deters frivolous litigation. Although many attorneys are honorable people, as in any profession there are some unscrupulous lawyers out there. As mentioned, with a system that rewards lawyers quite well for taking on large net-worth individuals, you need to take every step you can to protect your assets as best you can. Be assured, lawyers and their staffs have ways of finding out what assets you own. (It is incredible what you can learn about someone on the Internet.) So it is important to take steps to keep your name off public records, use entities that are not tied to you and take ownership in a form that is difficult to reach.

Asset Protection and Your Primary Residence

LLCs and LPs are excellent vehicles for holding real estate, as will be further discussed in Chapter Nine. What about using an LLC or LP for the asset protection of your primary residence?

Until recently, many homeowners were hesitant to use a protected entity to hold their primary residence for fear of losing certain key tax benefits. The IRS has cleared up these issues to the homeowner's advantage, thus accelerating the use of LLCs (but not LPs) for holding principal residences.

The first issue had to do with the mortgage interest deduction on homes. A key write-off for many homeowners, it cannot be taken through an entity. But with a single-member LLC (which can include husband and wife as joint tenants or their living trust) considered a disregarded entity for tax purposes, the mortgage interest deduction can flow directly onto the individuals tax return. A limited partnership, which by definition must have at least two separate partners, cannot be taxed as a single-member entity and therefore won't work for this important deduction.

A second key tax benefit has to do with the IRS's allowance of homeowners to take a tax-free gain of up to $500,000 for married couples filing jointly, or $250,000 for single persons on the sale of a personal residence. This major tax benefit has surprisingly few requirements. You have to have lived in the house for two out of the last five years. You don't have to be of a certain age or buy another house, as with the previous law. Instead, this tax-free gain is available to all homeowners. Many people are now buying fixer-uppers, living in them and improving them for two years, selling the house to obtain the tax-free gain and moving onto the next home.

A question existed as to whether the tax-free treatment was available to homeowners who held their property in the name of an LLC for asset protection purposes. After all, with all the improvements and fixing up going on with these properties, a measure of asset protection made a great deal of sense.

The IRS has recently come out with regulations indicating that the tax-free primary residence gains are available to homeowners who hold title in the name of an LLC. Be sure to work with your CPA on these issues but know that this allowance is a huge reason why more and more homeowners are placing their primary residences into an LLC.

As a result of this change, I have had clients ask whether they should use one LLC to hold both their primary residence and one or more rental properties. My answer is no. I would use a separate LLC for your primary residence, and not mix your home in with other properties. Above all, we want to protect your primary residence. Exposing it to the risks of your other properties is not at all suggested. That said, a properly-formed and current LLC holding your primary residence (and only your primary residence) is an excellent asset protection strategy for a very important asset.

In summary, the Limited Partnership or LLC interest is one of the best ways to hold ownership for the protection of certain assets, including real estate, brokerage accounts and intellectual property. When the ambulance-chasing or Mercedes-chasing attorney sees that your assets are in LP or LLC form – or better yet sees no assets – he or she will think hard about pursuing a case against you. Any step taken to deter frivolous litigation can bring peace of mind. Assets held by an LP or LLC are an excellent step in the direction of asset protection.

Frequently Asked Questions

What is the reasoning behind the charging order?

The charging order was designed to protect the partnership and the other partners. To allow a creditor direct access to a partnership's assets would disrupt the business of the partnership. Instead, a court-ordered charging order directing the partnership to make any distributions a partner would receive payable to the partner's creditors is seen as a less disruptive means of collection.

What interest rights does a creditor have with a charging order?

The creditor has the rights of an assignee of a partnership interest. Such an assignee does not have the ability to force a general partner to make a distribution. An assignee may only receive a distribution that the previous interest holder would have received.

What are the general partner/manager's duties to an assignee?

In most states, a general partner/manager owes few fiduciary duties to an assignee. In many states an assignee has no rights to an accounting or rights to a surplus.

Can the charging order protection be lost?

Yes, by placing assets into an LLC/LP in advance of or during litigation, a fraudulent conveyance may occur. In such cases, a creditor may reach the property by having the transfer voided or by attaching the transferred property.

What happens if a court allows a foreclosure and sale of a partner/member's interest?

First of all, only the partner/member's interest is sold, not the specific assets of the entity. Second, such an interest is not likely to command a high price, due to the limitations of the interest. If the creditor buys the interest they only are entitled to what they were receiving to begin with, the charged partner/member's profits.

Can the remaining partners/members take any steps prior to a foreclosure sale?

Yes. They may redeem the charged interest with their own property or, if all consent, with entity property. Or they may dissolve the entity and buy back the assets upon liquidation. An accounting must be given to the creditor for the charged interest of the debtor interest-holder.

Can a Homestead be used on a personal residence held by an LLC?

Many states require that a homestead only be used for a personal residence properly held in an individual name, thus precluding homesteading a personal residence held in an LLC. Check with your local advisor. A summary of state homestead laws can be found at www.successdna.com

Can a Buy-Sell Agreement be used to require the purchase of a charged interest?

Yes. A well-drafted agreement can require that a debtor partner/member sell their interest to the remaining interest-holders or the entity, thus avoiding the issue of an assignee's involvement.

How does the charging order apply to Nevada and Wyoming LLCs?

The charging order is the exclusive remedy by which a judgment creditor of a member of an LLC may charge a member's interest with payment of an unsatisfied amount of the judgment in both Nevada (NRS 86.01) and Wyoming (W.S. 7-15-145).

How does the charging order apply to Nevada and Wyoming LPs?

Again, the charging order is the exclusive remedy a judgment creditor has under Nevada law (NRS 88.535). In Wyoming the law states that the court may charge the partnership interest of a partner but is silent as to whether the charging order is the exclusive remedy or not (W.S. 17-14-803).

Do many people use Nevada or Wyoming LLCs to hold brokerage accounts?

Yes, with the advent of online brokerage accounts many people use a Nevada or Wyoming LLC (or LP) to hold stocks, bonds and securities accounts for asset protection purposes. Because the two states have no state taxes and the annual fees are very reasonable (only $50 a year in Wyoming), many brokerage accounts are held in asset-protected LLCs. The LLC offers the flexibility of moving money in and out of the brokerage account without extra taxation and, with the proper professional nominee relationship, the privacy that many citizens desire. As well, when setting up an LLC brokerage account, you can switch the shares from your name to the LLC without tax, since you are not selling the shares but merely transferring them to your own entity.

At what dollar amount do people set up LLCs or LPs to hold brokerage accounts?

Although there is no one correct figure or dividing line, many people set up Wyoming LLCs (due to their affordability) for brokerage accounts valued at $20,000 or more. Because Wyoming has a small franchise tax on assets used in Wyoming valued at $1 million or more, clients will consider using a Nevada LLC for million dollar plus brokerage accounts, or have the Wyoming LLC's brokerage account administered by a brokerage office located outside of the state of Wyoming.

Chapter Eight
Estate Planning and LLCs/LPs

In the next thirty years, several trillion dollars worth of assets will be transferred from one generation to the next. That is not a typo. It is trillions, not billions. It will be the largest transfer of wealth in the history of mankind. Given the enormity of this issue, the importance of proper estate planning cannot be overstated. The consequences of a lack of planning, such as seeing your valuable and hard-won estate be dissipated by unprepared or unworthy family members, or lost to a rapacious estate tax regime, make the need to understand certain surprisingly simple estate planning strategies all the more important.

First, some background information is appropriate. Estate planning is the planning for distribution of your wealth after your death. All citizens automatically have an estate plan, although, since it arises by default, it is not usually the one they want. Unless you have drafted and implemented a Will or Trust, your state of residence has a plan for the distribution of your assets, known as "intestate succession" (intestate means to die without a Will.) These rules amount to a family checklist of who stands first, second or third in line to receive your estate if you pass without drafting a Will. Interestingly, if no family members show up, most states wind up with your estate.

Again, most default situations do not satisfy specific needs. If you want to ensure that your wealth will benefit the people or organizations you care about, you will need a Will. Additionally, if you want to avoid the cost and other pitfalls of Probate, or if you want to minimize the taxes that will be imposed on your estate after your death, you will need a Trust.

Probate is a court-supervised process for the distribution of assets, which you hold in your name alone, or in a form that does not automatically transfer title to someone else at your death, such as joint tenancy. Probate requires hiring an attorney to represent your estate. The process usually takes from nine months to two years to get through or be "settled," depending on the circumstances. Probate fees can range from a few thousand to tens of thousands of dollars in some cases. Probate generally is required if you have a Will, if you have property in your name alone or if you have a Trust that is not properly structured and funded (i.e. title was not transferred from your individual name into the name of the Trust).

A Living Trust, also known as a Revocable Trust, is a Trust with terms and conditions that can be changed, terminated or revoked to meet changing needs. All property placed inside the Trust is managed by your Trustee (which can be you during your lifetime) and distributed at your death by your appointed Trustee without the need for a Probate. This is because assets that are placed into the Trust are not subject to Probate.

Funding the Trust is a crucial step and involves retitling assets from your name to the name of the Trust. Living Trusts usually provide that the income of the Trust is paid to you at period intervals, and you reserve the right to take out as much of the principal as you need during your lifetime.

Most Living Trusts are set up by individuals or couples who name themselves to serve as Trustee while they are alive and legally competent, with provisions for someone else, usually another relative, to serve as Trustee once they die or become incapacitated. In this way, your affairs will continue to be managed by someone you trust, without the need for guardianship or conservatorship proceedings. Because Trusts are private documents, which in most states are not filed with the court, your privacy is maintained through a Trust.

Properly drafted Living Trusts with spendthrift provisions can, in some cases, also place assets beyond the reach of creditors. With a "spendthrift" being a person who wastes money, a spendthrift trust contains protections against such waste and imprudence for the ultimate benefit of the wasteful beneficiary. In most states, a beneficiary's creditors cannot reach Trust assets if the power to distribute Trust assets is subject to the Trustee's discretion, provided the Trustee and the beneficiary are not the same person. Certain states, such as Nevada, offer Asset Protection Trusts, (sometimes known as Wealth Management Trusts), which can be very useful in protecting assets from future claimants. For more information on these Trusts visit www.sutlaw.com.

Another popular use of the Living Trust is to defer, reduce or avoid altogether federal estate taxes that would otherwise be imposed at your death. For 2004, there is no federal estate tax imposed on estates valued at $1.5 million or less. This "unified credit" amount will be increased to $2 million in 2006-2008 and $3.5 million in 2009. However, the marginal tax rates on estates valued above these amounts varies, from 37 percent to 55 percent. Presently, when one spouse dies, no federal estate tax is due, because one spouse can leave all of his or her estate to the other spouse, tax free, through the use of the Unlimited Marital Deduction. However, when the second spouse dies, the entire estate is subject to federal estate tax.

Without any basic tax planning, only the unified credit amount of the value of the estate can be excluded from federal estate taxation. With even minimal tax planning, an estate valued at twice that amount can be transferred free of federal estate tax by including provisions in the Living Trust for the creation of a Family Trust (also called a Credit Shelter Trust, or Exemption Equivalent Trust). Thus, significant taxes can be saved just by using a Living Trust. Through the use of other tax planning techniques, larger amounts can be exempted from federal estate taxation.

It was mentioned earlier that in the spring of 2001, Congress passed a bill that phases in a repeal of estate taxes with a full repeal in effect by 2010. However, the bill also provides that, unless Congress makes the repeal permanent, estate taxes of 55 percent will return on January 1, 2011. This type of half-hearted lawmaking creates huge problems for individuals and estate planners. How can you properly plan when the estate tax is zero one day and 55 percent the next? Unless amended, this law will make the last week of December

2010, a dangerous time. Voluntary – and involuntary – euthanasia will be prevalent. A number of elderly wealthy individuals will not ring in the New Year 2011, whether they want to or not. And Congress will again have failed to appreciate the very human dynamic between taxes and greed, when an estate owes nothing on December 31st and then millions and millions of dollars on January 1st.

A related issue regarding taxes and human motivation has to do with state inheritance taxes. The state you live in may affect how much you will have to pay in taxes. Many have relocated for this very reason. As an example, Nevada imposes no estate or inheritance tax on its residents. It also does not tax the income of its individuals, Corporations or other business interests. To the extent your place of residence has a state inheritance tax, you are better off in a tax-free state. A recent change in federal law also eliminated the "source tax", a particular bane of retired persons, which used to allow states like California to tax the pension and retirement plan distributions of its former residents who had moved to tax-free states like Nevada and Wyoming.

To summarize this estate planning overview:

1. If you care how your assets are distributed and about proceeds being reduced by expensive probate costs, create an estate plan and avoid your state's rules of intestate succession
2. To avoid Probate and to reduce federal estate taxes, a Living Trust should be formed and properly funded
3. As Trustee of your own Living Trust, you control your assets. But, because a Living Trust is revocable – cancelable or changeable at will – it offers no asset protection. A court can order you, as the Trustee, to revoke the Trust and turn over its assets
4. To achieve asset protection within an estate plan, the Living Trust can hold interests in a domestic Limited Partnership, LLC or other asset-protection entity

Limited Partnerships and LLCs are excellent entities to use as estate planning tools. Both are able to deal with the two major issues of estate planning:

1. Control.
2. Taxes.

First, to get the least pleasant issue out of the way at the start, we will deal with taxes. As mentioned, for the years 2004 and 2005, the first $1.5 million of a person's estate is excluded from estate taxes. Anything over $1.5 million is taxed at federal estate tax rates as high as 55 percent. The strategy then is to gift family assets to children and other relatives so that when the parents pass on, the estate is depleted and thus not subject to the very significant estate taxes. As reviewed in our case below, a gifting plan is therefore implemented, whereby gifts of these assets are made on an annual basis to reduce the estate's value. And while Congress would like you to believe that estate taxes have been repealed as of 2010, they really haven't, so gifting is just as important as ever.

It is important to understand that these gifts are to be made year after year over time. The IRS – for all its faults and fallacies – is not run by stupid people. They are actually quite smart at what they try to do, which is to fund their parent and patron, the federal government. So, when Congress authorizes a tax on the value of your estate at death, the IRS' first reaction is how to close any and all loopholes that the sharp lawyers and accountants of the world would use to avoid the estate tax. Hence, the gift tax.

Think about this from the IRS' view of things. If there is an estate tax of 55 percent on the value of a $10 million estate, the IRS asks: "What would a sophisticated millionaire on his deathbed do?" The answer: Two days before he dies, he will give away all of his assets to his children, to avoid the estate tax. So, the IRS came up with a way to prevent that from happening by instituting a gift tax, which is a tax on gifts made during one's life at the same rate as the estate tax. In this way, our sophisticated deathbed millionaire has to pay the same amount of tax to the IRS whether he gifts his assets during his life or at his death. You can easily envision the high fives at the IRS when this loophole was closed.

However, a blanket tax on all gifts to all persons in all situations would be nearly impossible – as well as very unpleasant, even for the IRS – to enforce. The IRS, according to popular legend, has defined its role as plucking the feathers from a live chicken without the chicken squawking. One can only imagine the squawking if the IRS tried to assert a gift tax on the $100 a father gave his sons to go to a baseball game, or the $20 a grandmother gave her grandchild in a birthday card. Both are gifts. Both could be taxed under the gift tax law regime.

To avoid the squawking, the IRS set an exclusion of $11,000 per year per person from the gift tax. A father and mother then can give up to $11,000 to each of their children. Assuming they have four children, a total of $88,000 can be gifted each year, but there is no limit on the number of children who may receive gifts. If their grandparents are so inclined, another $88,000 can be gifted to the four children. (Please note that if Grandma gifts $11,000 to her granddaughter in May as a part of her estate planning strategy, and then gives her another $100 as a Christmas present, technically that $100 may be subject to a gift tax of $18.)

So with a $11,000 gift tax exclusion in place, the estate planning strategy of gifting $11,000 from each spouse to each child on an annual basis was born. And with the ability for each spouse to gift (as in our example) to four children, a grand total of $88,000 could be gifted away every year (there is no limit on the amount of children that you may gift to).

But what if the parents have an estate valued at $4 million? With a gifting program of $88,000 per year, it would take 50 years to gift away this estate in allowable gifts from two spouses to their four children. And note, where there are only two children, the corresponding gift allowance reduces to $44,000, meaning that it would take over 90 years to gift away their estate. And further note that an estate worth $4 million today might appreciate to be worth $8 million ten years from now – further running out the time needed for gifting. Either the parents start gifting early (which almost never happens), or they must figure out a way to accelerate their gifting program.

Before illustrating how to accelerate gifting through the use of an LP or LLC, it should be noted that there are a number of estate planning techniques available. Some will be briefly addressed in the Frequently Asked Questions section at the end of this chapter. But because a complete review of the estate planning arena is beyond the scope of this book, please consider consulting with an estate planning attorney in your own area to develop and implement a strategy best suited for your individual situation.

Case Number 2 - Mary and Gary

Mary and Gary have formed G & M Properties, LP to hold a four-plex they have purchased for investment purposes. They have formed M & G Holdings, LP, to hold certain stock investments they have made. To manage each of the Limited Partnerships they form Woodside Management Corporation to own two percent of each Limited Partnership and serve as the corporate general partner, thus encapsulating the personal liability of the general partner in a corporate (or, had they wanted to, an LLC) entity. And, by using LPs in their home state of California, Mary and Gary avoided paying California's annoying gross receipts tax on LLC revenues.

The four-plex was purchased for $400,000 in cash. The building, while old, is located on a large lot in an appreciating downtown area going through a renaissance of redevelopment. It is reasonably believed that the land value alone will be worth $800,000 in the next 10 years. Mary and Gary want to distribute Limited Partnership interests to their four children before the asset appreciates up and away from their ability to gift it out.

To do so, they have the four-plex informally valued by a local realtor. While an independent real estate appraiser may charge $3,000 or more for such a report, all Mary and Gary need for their gifting program is a letter from an independent third party knowledgeable in the field as to the current market value. The broker who sold them the property knows the market and is happy to write such a letter on an annual basis for their file. He also appreciates the nice bottle of wine Mary and Gary give him every year as a thank-you gift. This token of appreciation is acceptable but their accountant reminds them that to be valid in the eyes of the IRS the appraiser must have no pecuniary interest in the outcome of any minority discount case. In addition, the expert must not rely on data furnished by the taxpayer but must rather conduct his own independent examination of the assets and the market.

In the first year of owning the property, Mary and Gary's broker's letter indicates that the market value is right at their purchase price, or $400,000. Mary and Gary are not upset the property has not yet greatly appreciated. They want the appraised value to be low so they can gift away a greater percentage interest to their children.

With four children, Amy, Charlie, Ellie and Haley, they can gift a total of $88,000 per year (two parents x four children x $11,000 per child). If the property does not increase in value and Mary and Gary do not use a valuation discount, they can gift the property to their children in just over four and one-half years. However, because the property is going to appreciate, and because Mary and Gary wanted to start gifting away their other Limited Partnership, M & G Holdings, LP, as well, they are keen to gift away G & M Properties, LP's Limited Partnership interests as soon as possible by taking as great a valuation discount as is practical.

First, Mary and Gary need to know more about valuation discounting. They learn from their accountant that gift and estate taxes are levied on the fair market value of the interest that is gifted during life or bequeathed at death. Fair market value for the purposes of assessing both taxes is defined as the price a willing buyer and a willing seller, both having knowledge of the relevant facts involved, and neither being forced to buy or sell, would be willing to accept. Fair market value can then be discounted and reduced for a lack of marketability or a lack of control.

A lack of marketability occurs when the property interest cannot be disposed of in an efficient manner – either due to restrictions on transfer found in the organizational documents, or due to external market factors. For example, a profitable retail business in Prudhoe Bay, Alaska, may suffer from an external lack of marketability because not everyone wants to live above the Arctic Circle.

A lack of control (or a minority discount) occurs when the interest to be purchased is not large enough to have control over the asset or business it represents. Buyers will not pay 40 percent of the fair market value of an asset when the 40 percent is represented by an interest that allows them no control. As an example, a commercial office building is worth $2 million. A 40 percent interest in the asset could be considered worth $800,000. But with the asset held in an LLC or an LP, the 40 percent ownership is in the entity – not the building itself – and does not give the control of selling the property. So the buyer is not going to pay $800,000 for a 40 percent interest that may be locked up and illiquid for years to come. Instead he or she is going to put $800,000 into owning a different office building where he or she has 100 percent control. Which means, in market terms, that the 40 percent interest in the first office building is going to have to be valued for a lot less to get anyone interested in investing. In a Limited Partnership setting, a buyer could purchase a 98 percent Limited Partnership interest and still not have control, due to a two percent General Partnership interest controlling the entire investment. A valuation discount for a lack of control is justified and accepted in such a circumstance.

As is evident, a lack of marketability and control are foundational features of Limited Partnerships and LLCs. These entities are used for the very reason that they offer restrictions on transferability and control. As such, they are the ideal entities for use in obtaining justifiable valuation discounts.

So instead of gifting $14,000 in cash directly to one child – and losing all control over how that child manages, or mismanages, the money – as well as paying a gift tax on $3,000 – by putting the money into a Limited Partnership, gifting a Limited Partnership interest to the child, and retaining a General Partnership interest, control is maintained. The $14,000 interest can be discounted, due to a lack of control and marketability to a value of $11,000, thus avoiding any gift tax.

Once this valuation technique is appreciated, the question always becomes: How much of a discount will the IRS allow? Is it 25 percent, 35 percent, or can you go as high as 65 percent? While there is no brightline test or number, the simple answer is found in this maxim: "Pigs get fat, hogs get slaughtered." If you get greedy with your discounting, the IRS can and will call into question all of your planning. In my practice I do not advise my clients to go over a 35 percent discount. I prefer to use a 30 percent discount. I have dealt with some professionals who, with absolute certainty, assert that higher discounts are justified. Again, there is no correct answer. But it is interesting to note that most court cases adjudicating discounting issues involve fact patterns in which taxpayers took discounts of 40 percent or more. Importantly, recent IRS cases have indicated a willingness to challenge discounts of more than 30 percent. This is an ever-changing area of the law, so be sure to deal with your tax advisor when delving into discounting.

Be sure also to review the Frequently Asked Questions section for the information that the IRS will request in the event it seeks to audit your Family Limited Partnership. It is instructive. Above all, you and your advisor should establish your own comfort level for gifting.

Back to Mary and Gary. They want to gift away G & M Properties, LP, as soon as possible. With the assistance of their accountant, they utilize the broker's letter to establish a value of $400,000 for the four-plex. As such, each one percent interest in the Limited Partnership is worth $4,000. However, because the Limited Partnership Agreement provides for restrictions on any transfer of interest and limits the limited partners' involvement in management and control, the two discounts for marketability and control justify a 30 percent reduction in value. Accordingly, each one percent interest is valued at $2,800 instead of $4,000. So, instead of only gifting two and three-quarter percent fair market value interests to each child (2.75 x $4,000 = $11,000), each spouse can gift three and ninety-three hundredths percent discounted interests to each child (3.93 x $2,800 = $11,000).

Mary and Gary's accountant says that minutes of a meeting should be prepared detailing and approving the gifts. Upon approval, new partnership certificates are to be issued whereby Mary and Gary's interest (held by their Living Trust) is reduced and the four children's interests (held by a custodian pursuant to the Uniform Gifts to Minors Act or, in some states, the Uniform Act on Transfers to Minors) are accordingly increased. Mary and Gary's accountant states that it is important to follow these formalities.

The annual result for four children is that instead of gifting 22 percent of the Limited Partnership interests, by discounting Mary and Gary give away 31.44 percent of the Limited Partnership interests each year to Amy, Charlie, Ellie, and newborn Haley. Assuming they want Woodside Management, the corporate general partner, to retain its two percent General Partnership interest in G & M Properties, Limited Partnership for control and management purposes, then a total of 98 percent is to be gifted. Without using a valuation discount the gifting will take 4.45 years. By taking a 30 percent discount, the gifting is completed in 3.12 years. When estates valued at even more money are involved, the difference in the number of years to accomplish the gifting can be even more significant.

However, Mary and Gary's accountant reminds them that the property valuation is not a constant. They need to base the value for gifting on a broker's letter of appraisal on an annual basis. If their property does not increase in value they can gift out all the Limited Partnership interests in 3.12 years. If, however, the property appreciates in value, it will take longer.

Then their accountant tells them about an interesting strategy for accelerated gifting. Assume that gifts have been made to Amy, Charlie, Ellie and Haley in year one. It is now the end of year two, and no gifts have been made, but the property continues to appreciate. In late December, Mary and Gary get the broker's letter estimating that the property is now worth $450,000. Privately, the broker tells the two of them that when certain properties sell the following spring, their four-plex will be worth more than $450,000. They need to gift their interests sooner rather than later.

Based on the broker's appraisal of $450,000 they value each one percent interest at $4,500. With a 30 percent discount, each one percent interest is worth $3,150. On December 30th of year two, each parent gifts 3.49 percent to each child (3.49 % x $3,150 per 1% interest = $11,000). With two spouses and four children, the aggregate gifted interest is 27.94 percent. When combined with the 31.44 percent interest gifted in year one, a total of 59.38 percent has now been transferred by Mary and Gary into their children's names. On January 2nd, three days after the year two gifts are made, but in a brand new tax year, another 27.94 percent interest is gifted. The property appraisal of $450,000 and the valuation of $3,150 per one percent interest may still be used in this year three gifting, because the appraisal is only two weeks old and thus current for year three.

Had Mary and Gary waited several months into year three to finish their gifting, they would have had to obtain a new broker's appraisal letter, thereby running the risk of having the four-plex valued at a higher rate. By gifting another 27.94 percent at the lowest rate, they have just over ten percent left to gift in year four and can start making additional gifts of other interests in year four.

Mary and Gary are glad to have completed the transfer of G & M Properties, LP, as they now want to focus their gifting of M & G Holdings LP. This Limited Partnership holds their securities portfolio and it appears that one very early-stage stock they have taken a flyer on is about to soar.

Their accountant has advised them that as of 2004 there will be a one-time gift exclusion of $1.5 million. This means that each spouse can make gifts totaling $1.5 million, free from gift or estate tax, once during their lifetime. But once they make the $1.5 million gift during their lifetime, the estate has no exclusions and is subject to tax on the first dollar. This was to be minimized with the Congressional phased-in repeal of estate taxes by 2010. However, Mary, Gary, their accountant and everyone else knew that they could not rely on this new law. But, the lifetime gift exclusion is appealing, because it allows them to remove $1.5 million from their estate in one fell swoop. It also does not prohibit them from continuing or implementing a gifting plan of $11,000 per person, per year. The $1.5 million lifetime gift is especially attractive for an appreciating asset. A real-estate investment worth $1.5 million today that is clearly going to be worth $10 million in five years, is a good candidate for such a one-time gift, especially since it would be very difficult to gift away a $10 million asset in $11,000 annual increments. While other estate planning techniques are available, including a charitable remainder trust, the one-time gift is a valuable technique. The downside is that once the gift is made, the exclusion is used up – even if the fair market value of the gift falls below $1.5 million.

Mary and Gary consider using the lifetime gift exclusion for their wildly appreciating stock. But having recently learned that a wild upturn can be followed by an even more dramatic downturn, they decide to save their $1.5 million free gift for later use. They continue gifting $88,000 per year to Amy,

Charlie, Ellie and Haley of M & G Holdings, LP Limited Partnership interests at the discounted rate.

LLCs and Estate Planning

For the purpose of our discussion so far, we have utilized a Limited Partnership. Many estate planners prefer to use Limited Partnerships due to the certainty of the management responsibility being exclusively controlled by the general partner, and the absolute prohibition of any management involvement whatsoever assigned to the limited partners.

For many planners, the LLC does not offer such certainty. Members may have the right to vote out managers and may also have the right to get involved in the business. A great deal will depend upon how each LLC's Operating Agreement is drafted. But certainly it will be difficult to assert a lack of control discount when an individual owns 60 percent of an LLC and the Operating Agreement provides that all managers may be replaced by a 55 percent vote of the members, or that all expenditures over $20,000 requires a 51 percent vote of the members. Under that scenario, the 60 percent LLC member effectively has management control and authority, for which the IRS would argue, with some justification, that no discount was available. Or see the South Dakota law discussed on page 237. There, a member can simply demand his money back. A lack of marketability discount is not fully justified under that law.

A solution that some planners use is to create two classes of LLC members. One class is akin to the general partner in a Limited Partnership. This class has exclusive rights to elect the manager and oversee the business. The second class has no voting rights whatsoever. Members of this class must sit back and take whatever the controlling class gives them, which while not politically tasteful, works for estate planning purposes. The key, however, is that the Operating Agreement must be drafted with care so as to eliminate any possible control benefits or rights for the non-voting class of members.

But for many conservative planners a nagging thought remains – that is, because the LLC is still a new entity, the courts have not yet fully interpreted LLC law. Unlike corporate or partnership law, there is not a several hundred-year-old body of case law fleshing out the rights, responsibilities and restrictions on LLC members. And so the question becomes: Will future court cases treat non-voting LLC members as limited partners where control is not a right, or as corporate non-voting shareholders, where certain rights and remedies are available? And if found to be akin to corporate law, or even somewhere in between corporate and partnership law – as some judge could somehow decide – how will future court cases impact the control issue for the discount valuation of LLCs?

Believe me, these seemingly arcane and esoteric issues are the ones that keep more than a few lawyers and accountants awake at night.

Therefore to completely avoid the issues of whether the LLC Operating Agreement has been perfectly drafted and whether some court somewhere someday may rule that non-voting LLC members still have control rights, thus negating justifiable discounts, some conservative planners will simply opt for the Limited Partnership over the LLC. For them, it is the easiest decision.

This is not necessarily a wrong decision. There is no one right answer for every situation. You and your advisors must review a number of factors and determine which strategy works best for you in your judgment. Be it an LP or an LLC for estate planning purposes, you must arrive at the entity with which you are most comfortable and begin gifting. A key point of this chapter is that both Limited Partnerships and LLCs can be excellent tools for estate planning purposes, and that to accomplish your estate planning goals through gifting you may want to start sooner rather than later.

Frequently Asked Questions

If I have a Living Trust and want to hold and gift assets from an LP or an LLC, how should I hold the partner or member interests?

You should hold and gift assets in the name of the Living Trust. A chart helps to illustrate the relationship.

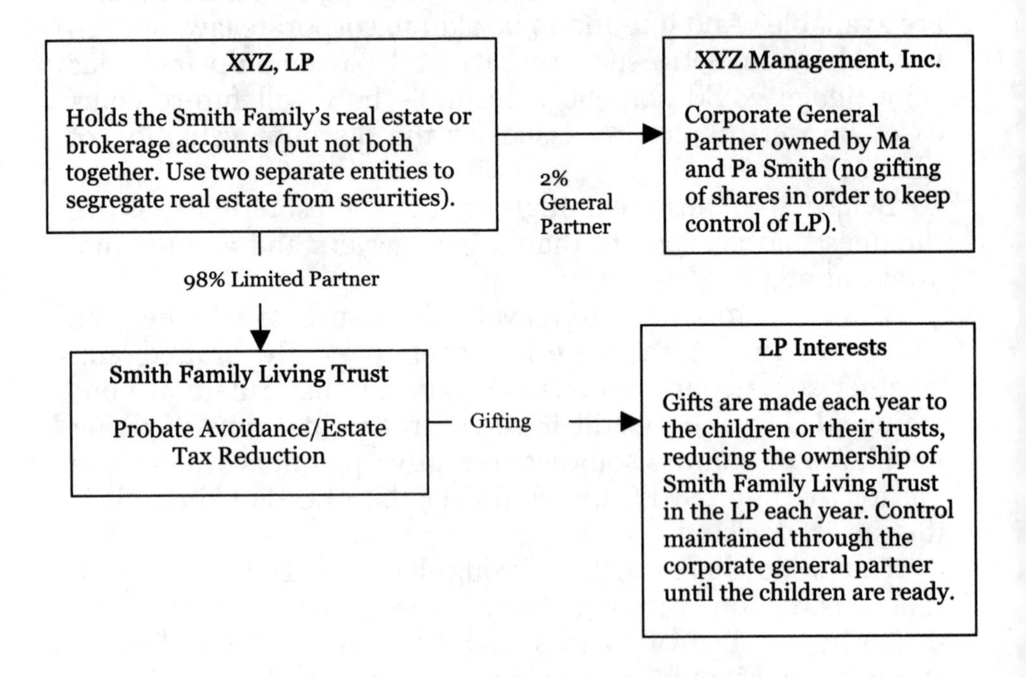

Are LLCs and LPs more favorable for estate planning purposes than Trusts?

In terms of taxes, LLCs and LPs may be more favorable. With Trusts, at a taxable income of just less than $10,000 the highest marginal tax rate is achieved with respect to income that is not distributed or not required to be distributed. Because income is passed through to LLC members and LP limited partners, the tax obligation may be lower with those entities than a Trust. As an example, if $20,000 flowed through an LLC to a children's Trust the tax would be $6,900. The child receiving the money directly would pay $4,000 less in tax.

My wife and I have an LP that holds rental properties. We now want to gift to our children. Should we gift to them directly or to a Trust?

As mentioned above, in terms of taxes, a Trust may be less tax efficient. In terms of control, a Trust may offer superior benefits, especially if parents want assets to be out of reach until their children reach age 25 or older. The gifted LP interest can be a satisfactory device, given its tax efficiency and control benefits.

Are LLCs and LPs more favorable for estate planning purposes than Sub-Chapter S Corporations?

Limited Partnerships, LLCs and certain Trusts cannot be shareholders of a Sub-Chapter S Corporation. Thus, business succession planning with Sub-Chapter S Corporations is limited because owners can't transfer shares to the kind of entities (LLCs, LPs and Trusts) needed to provide control and discounting opportunities. Transferring shares of a Sub-Chapter S Corporation (without discounting) to children over time may also result in them having control of the company before they are ready for such a responsibility.

How should minor children hold their gifted membership or Limited Partnership interests?

Under the Uniform Gift to Minors Act or the Uniform Act on Transfers to Minors, in most states it is possible to transfer a membership or partnership interest to a custodian who will hold the interest until the minor becomes 18 or 21 or later, if provided for in a Will or Trust, up to age 25. It is advisable to check your state's statute, since a few may not allow such interests to be held and may provide for different holding periods. A Trust may also be used to hold such interests. If irrevocable, a Trust can provide creditor protection, including protection from divorce and imprudent spending habits.

What is the effect on the LLC and the members' LLC interests upon the death of a member and the effect on the LP and the limiteds' partnership interest upon the death of a limited?

The Operating Agreement or Partnership Agreement may or may not be drafted to provide for a dissolution and liquidation of the LLC or LP upon an interest-holder's death. If you want the membership or partnership interests to continue despite an interest holder's death, you should draft the agreement to so provide. Some state's default rules will otherwise provide for a dissolution. It may be important that the entity does not dissolve and liquidate at one's death if gifting with a discount plan in place. It would be hard to convince the IRS that a minority/marketability discount was justified during a liquidation of all the assets.

On the other hand, a situation could exist where the founder/contributor to an LLC/LP wanted the entity to dissolve upon the death of an interest holder. For example, a father knows his second wife and eldest daughter will never get along as residents of the same planet, much less interest holders in the same entity. The Agreement may be drafted so that the entity is liquidated upon the father's death.

What is the difference between a Limited Partnership and a Family Limited Partnership?

A Family Limited Partnership is used to describe a Limited Partnership that holds family assets. Legally, there is no difference between the two. Both are Limited Partnerships subject to the same statutory and taxation requirements.

What is a Charitable Remainder Trust?

A Charitable Remainder Trust (CRT) is an irrevocable (unchangeable) split interest Trust into which specific assets are placed. The benefits are split, whereby the income or annuity portion goes to a beneficiary for a fixed period and upon expiration the remainder benefits go to a charitable organization. A Charitable Lead Trust is the reverse, with the charity receiving the income stream first. There are significant income tax and estate tax benefits associated with such Trusts.

What is an Irrevocable Life Insurance Trust?

An Irrevocable Life Insurance Trust is used to ensure that life insurance proceeds on a decedent's death are not subject to estate taxes while providing a source of liquidity to pay the decedent's estate taxes. A source of liquidity (readily available cash) is important to prevent a distressed or fire sale of assets to pay the estate taxes, which are due within nine months of death.

Does a gift of a future interest in a Limited Partnership or LLC qualify for the $11,000 annual gift tax exclusion?

No, the gift must be of a present, readily valuable interest. The IRS has held that gifts of corporate stock subject to a 10-year restriction on transfer are future interests. Nevertheless, gifts of Limited Partnership interests, which are subject to a right of first refusal by other limited partners before or after a transfer can occur, have been held to be present interests.

Must one claiming a valuation discount notify the IRS?

Yes, the gift tax return, IRS Form 709, requires taxpayers to state whether a valuation discount is being used. Supporting information must be supplied. As such, it is important to properly document the transaction. In addition, by filing the return, the statute of limitations begins to run. If there is a question as to valuation, the IRS has three years from the due date of the return, including extensions, to object. If no return is filed, the issue of valuation remains open.

What if a gift is $11,000 or less?

No filing is required if the gift is less than $11,000. However, as mentioned above, you may want to file to take advantage of the three-year statute of limitations.

What information will the IRS request if they decide to audit your Family Limited Partnership?

What follows is a fairly onerous request for documents that the IRS used in one case. As such, please note that the IRS may not use this request in every situation. Some of the requested information could also be protected under the attorney-client privilege if an attorney was used, or resisted on the grounds of relevance to an audit. Nevertheless, if you and your advisors are going to engage in aggressive gifting, it is useful to know what the IRS will want to see in an audit situation.

1. All documents relating to the creation of the partnership (including bills) from any attorney, accountant or firm involved in recommending the creation of the partnership or in drafting the Partnership Agreement. If a claim is made that any of these documents are privileged, identify each privileged document by date, source, audience and reason for the privilege.
2. Original Partnership Agreement and all amendments thereto.
3. Articles of Incorporation of the general partner, if the general partner is a Corporation.
4. All documents that were prepared to meet state law requirements on the formation and operation of the partnership (i.e., Certificate of Limited Partnership with

the filing date stamp on it and all amendments thereto, stamped copies of annual reports; supplemental affidavits on capital contributions, etc.).

5. All partnership financial statements and tax returns prepared and/or filed since inception.

6. All of the partnership's bank and other records (i.e., general ledger, cash receipts and disbursements, journals, check registers, etc.) which reflect the amount and nature of all deposits and distributions, including distributions to partners, for the period since the partnership was formed to the date of death/current date.

7. Minutes of all partnership meetings; if none, indicate the dates of all meetings and the business discussed.

8. Evidence showing how the value of each partnership asset was arrived at as of the date:

(a) it was contributed to the partnership;

(b) of each gift of a partnership interest; and

(c) of the death of the donor; provide all appraisals and supporting work papers obtained of the partnership's assets, including partnership interests and any discounts.

9. Evidence to substantiate all initial and subsequent capital contributions and the source of all contributions by partners other than the donor/decedent.

10. For any partnership asset that has been sold or offered for sale since the formation of the partnership, provide evidence to document the sale or attempted sale (i.e., sale agreement, listing agreement, escrow statement, etc.).

11. For each partnership asset, explain/provide:

(a) evidence that the partnership owns the asset (i.e., deeds, bills of sale, other title changes and account statements);

(b) when the donor/decedent acquired the asset;

(c) how the asset was used by the donor/decedent since its acquisition and how the partnership has used the asset since (i.e., held for rent, personal residence, investment, etc.); and

(d) who managed the asset prior to and after its contribution; explain in detail what the management consisted of and how it changed after the partnership was formed.

12. Brokerage statements reflecting the ownership and activity of the securities and mutual funds contributed to the partnership for the period beginning one year prior to the formation of the partnership and continuing through the current date, and copies of any other tax returns and financial statements, which reflect the activity of the partnership assets, if different from the foregoing.

13. For each gift or transfer of a partnership interest, provide:

(a) evidence that the partnership interest was legally transferred under state law and under the Partnership Agreement;

(b) any assignment of partnership interest prepared;

(c) the terms of the assignment, if not indicated in a written assignment;

(d) the amount and source of any consideration paid; and

(e) an explanation of how the amount of the consideration was arrived at.

14. Provide the following with respect to the donor/decedent, all other original partners and any recipients of gifts or transfers of partnership interests:

(a) date of birth;

(b) education and occupation;

(c) experience and expertise in dealing with partnerships, real estate, financial affairs and investments; provide tangible evidence thereof;

(d) extent of the donor's/decedent's investments as of the date of the formation of the partnership, including a summary of assets that were not contributed to the partnership; provide tangible evidence thereof; and

(e) any personal financial statements and credit applications which were prepared in connection with loan applications after the partnership was created.

15. Indicate whether the partnership is currently in existence, and if so, provide the current ownership interests.

16. Provide a summary of any other transfers of partnership interests not reflected in the gift tax returns filed.

17. A statement describing the donor's/decedent's state of health at the time of the formation of the partnership and for the six-month period prior thereto, including a description of any serious illnesses. Please also provide the names, addresses and telephone numbers of all doctors who would have knowledge of the donor's/decedent's state of health during this period to the present date and provide these doctors with authorization to respond to the Service's future requests for information, including a copy of the medical records, if necessary.

18. The donor's/decedent's Will, Revocable Trust and any executed power of attorney, if not submitted with the return.

19. A statement indicating the identity of the parties recommending the use of the partnership, when the recommendations were made and the reasons set forth in support of the partnership.

20. Names, addresses and current telephone numbers of the representatives of the donor/estate, all donees/beneficiaries, all partners, accountants, bookkeepers and brokers/investment advisors.

Chapter Nine
Real Estate

LLCs and LPs are generally considered the vehicles of choice for holding real estate. In fact, the rule of thumb that Corporations should not own real estate is due to the fact that LLCs and LPs are such superior entities for this purpose.

First off, it must be noted that the ownership of real estate involves certain risks and thus exposure to personal liability. Owning rental real estate means that tenants may sue for real or imagined grievances. Owning vacant land means that, at the extreme end, trespassers may sue for hazardous conditions. (If you own vacant land and decide not to put it into an LLC or LP, at the very least obtain individual umbrella insurance coverage and list the vacant lot's parcel number as a coverage item.) Real estate may also involve personal liability for leases, contracts and mortgages as well as for expensive environmental remediation and clean up.

That said, the need for limiting one's liability is apparent. Corporations can accomplish this, of course. But there is one significant area with regard to real estate where Corporations fall short compared to LLCs and LPs and for most accountants is the reason why Corporations should not hold real estate. The issue involves the distribution (to members, partners or shareholders) of appreciated real property.

<u>Case Number 2 – Mary and Gary</u>

Prior to their estate plan gifting program and their understanding of LLC and LP law, Mary and Gary had wrestled with how to take title. As we now know, they had located a four-plex in an appreciating area. Knowing that they wanted asset protection and a limitation of liability they considered forming either an LP, LLC or Corporation to hold the real estate. Their accountant tells them that if they ever want to distribute an appreciated real estate asset out of an entity they formed the consequences would be significantly different for each entity.

Mary and Gary's first reaction is: Why would we want to transfer the asset out of the entity we formed? A good question, their accountant notes. He then explains that if Mary and Gary are ever to sell the property, most lawyers representing buyers will not want to assume whatever liabilities, whatever skeletons or unknowns, are associated with the LLC, LP or Corporation. Most lawyers, in trying to protect their buyer/client will want to buy only the asset (the real property) and not the entity, which may have claims or contingent liabilities against it that the buyer could then become unwittingly responsible for.

So the ability to hold the real estate in a protected vehicle is the first half of the equation, with the second half being the ability to get it out cleanly so it can be sold to the next guy.

Mary and Gary's accountant outlines the following tax scenario for distributing out appreciated real estate. Assume that the adjusted tax basis of the real estate is $100,000 and the fair market value is $500,000. If the property has been held long-term (over one year) the consequences are as follows:

C Corporation: The $400,000 gain is taxed first at the corporate tax rate. Approximately $136,000 is paid in tax. The gain on a non-liquidating distribution of the remaining $264,000 is then taxed again as a dividend to the shareholders. The current rate of dividends is 15 percent, leaving the shareholders with only $224,400 left.

If they liquidate (dissolve) the C Corporation, the tax consequence formula is as follows:

Sale Proceeds:	$ 400,000
Tax Payable	- 136,000
Subtotal	264,000
Less: Basis	- 50,000
Capital Gain	214,000
Less: Tax (Capital Gains)	-32,100
REMAINDER:	$181,900

Clearly, holding real estate in a C Corporation carries a sizeable tax burden. What are the alternatives?

Sub-Chapter S Corporation: The $400,000 gain passes through the corporate level without tax and is taxed at the shareholder's individual capital gain rate.

LLC or LP: Similarly, the $400,000 gain flows through the LLC or LP to its members or partners where it is taxed at their individual capital gain rate.

Due to the flow-through nature of S Corporations and LLCs/LPs, each entity will have the same net tax consequences when the property is sold. But the real benefit of using an LLC or LP to hold real estate comes when the owners want to remove the property from the entity without selling it, or want to convert it to personal use property. For example, Mary and Gary own the above-mentioned four-plex. They decide that they want to deal with a higher class of tenant, so they enter into a like-kind (tax free) exchange of the four-plex for a $500,000 home in an upscale neighborhood. They rent the home for a couple of years. Realizing that they are tired of the upscale tenants' whims and idiosyncrasies, they decide to convert the rental into personal use property and live in it as their primary personal residence. At the end of the day, if Gary and Mary owned the four-plex in an LLC, they would now own a $500,000 home and be able to enjoy the good life without any tax consequence on the conversion from business to personal property. If the four-plex were owned in an S Corporation, getting the home out of the S Corporation would have resulted in a significant tax liability. Couldn't you think of better things to do than paying a tax bill just because you wanted to put real property in an S Corporation?

Still talking to their accountant, Mary and Gary also learn that loan refinancing proceeds can be distributed tax-free by an LLC or LP, but that, again, a Corporation can not do so. He notes that this could be important if they ever want to access cash quickly by tapping into their real estate's equity through refinancing.

LLC or LP?

The question for Mary or Gary then becomes whether to use an LLC or LP to hold the real estate.

Their accountant points out a subtle tax difference between the two entities involving recourse debt. When an entity borrows money, many lenders will ask for a personal guarantee from one or all of the members, partners or shareholders. If the entity doesn't pay, the lenders want recourse (the ability to collect from someone else, such as a personal guarantor). In some cases, the entity or its assets are so strong that a lender may not seek a personal guarantee, in which case the loan to the entity is considered a non recourse debt.

The issue arises with regard to a party's tax basis. By including an entity's debt in your tax basis you can use up a greater amount of the entity's losses to offset other sources of income. As an example, assume you and two friends purchased a duplex for $120,000 with $30,000 down and a loan of $90,000. If your share of the purchase price is $10,000 you can write off losses generated by the entity up to that amount. However, if you can also include your share of the value of the loan (debt) in your tax basis, in this case $30,000, you can write off a total of $40,000 in losses (your $10,000 down plus the loan share of $30,000) in order to offset other income you may have. It should be noted that S Corporation shareholders cannot include in the basis of their stock the Corporation's debt, assuming the debt is qualified non-recourse financing.

With an LP, by definition, a general partner is personally liable for any debt. And the wrinkle in all of this is that because of the general partner's automatic liability (whether the debt is recourse or not) the limited partners cannot increase their tax basis by the debt unless they personally guarantee the debt. Many limited partners may not want to take on a personal guarantee, especially if they do not really have to otherwise. As such, if real property is purchased with recourse debt, all the LLC members receive an increase in basis, while in the LP setting only the general partner(s) get any increase in basis.

Back to Mary and Gary. They are not going to borrow any money to purchase the four-plex. While they appreciate knowing the rules on recourse debt, they are going to pay cash. Their tax basis is going to be the current fair market value of the property anyway. They want to know what other considerations there are in using an LLC versus an LP.

Their accountant then discusses one other main issue: management and its cost.

As we have discussed, LLC members can either be active or passive in their management. With an LP, only the general partner may manage. It is advisable to use a Corporation or an LLC to serve as the general partner in order to limit liability. But then you are paying the annual state's filing and tax return preparation fees for two entities instead of one.

For Mary and Gary, the additional cost is not material. They like the definitive mandate of a Limited Partnership, whereby limited partners can in no way be involved in management. They like using an LP for their estate plan gifting strategy. Because they live in California they also like staying away from the State of California's extra taxes on LLCs. Their accountant indicates that each client is different, with some favoring the reduced expense of an LLC and the need to only prepare one entity tax return.

To each his own entity.

Frequently Asked Questions

Can an entity own real estate?

Yes. Both LPs and LLCs may own real estate and are frequently formed for that purpose.

Who gets the mortgage interest deduction when property is held in an entity?

Some courts have held that the mortgage interest deduction for primary residences is available only to individuals, not entities. However, many accountants now use a single-member LLC, which is a disregarded entity for tax purposes, to flow-through the deduction onto your personal return. Be sure to check with your own accountant on this issue. Also consider the two cases in California and Colorado that deprived single-member LLCs of complete asset-protection benefits.

Can I receive the benefits of a homestead exemption on property held in an LLC/LP?

It depends upon your state's statute. Frequently, homesteads are only allowed for individuals, and in some older statutes only for a husband and wife, thus precluding entity ownership. Be sure to check with a professional in your area before transferring real estate.

Can an LLC/LP hold my primary residence?

Yes. See the discussion on page 154 for this useful strategy.

Does a transfer of real estate into an entity trigger a due-on-sale clause for mortgages?

Many mortgages are written so that any transfer will technically trigger a due-on-sale clause requiring the borrower to pay off the full amount of the loan. By law, however, mortgage companies have to allow a transfer from a borrower to a Living Trust so that the borrower can achieve his or her estate planning goals. I have had clients explain in advance to the mortgage company that they are first going to transfer the property into a Living Trust and from there transfer it into an LLC/LP so that they can further accomplish their estate planning and gifting goals. When the mortgage company agrees they then explain that because there are often transfer taxes and other costs associated with it all they are just going to do one transfer, from their individual name to the LLC/LP. In most cases, this works. I have had other clients consciously risk that the mortgage company's computer will never notice a transfer as long as the mortgage is paid and transfer away without notice to anyone. A key factor in the due-on-sale question is whether interest rates are in balance or not. If older rates are at seven percent and newer rates are at 12 percent you can be sure that mortgage companies will be out looking for ways to trigger due-on-sale clauses so they can lend money at higher rates.

I want to buy real estate in the name of an LLC/LP but lenders won't loan to my new entity. What can be done?

Many lenders will not loan monies to a newly formed LLC/LP entity created for the purpose of acquiring real estate. Look at it from the lender's point of view: the entity is brand new, with no track record and no assets. Would you lend to such a client? However, there is a way to achieve your goal. Lenders will allow you, as an individual, to borrow the money to buy the real estate. Title is taken in your name. Several days later title is transferred into the entity's name, offering the protection you need. The lender can hold you personally responsible for the loan, which is what they need.

What is the proper way to hold real estate assets when using an LLC/LP?

Real estate assets should be held in the name of the entity. On the county recorders' rolls for example, Parcel 123-456 should be titled to XYZ, LLC (or XYZ, LP). Failure to so hold such an asset may allow a creditor to reach it on the grounds that proper formalities were not followed.

How does a transfer of real property into an LLC/LP affect title insurance?

There can be certain situations in which title insurance protection will not apply to a new entity or the successor of a dissolved entity. You should review the terms of any title insurance policy carefully prior to any transfer. As a general rule you will want to use a grant deed instead of quit claim deed in an attempt to preserve the title insurance.

Is a real estate LP or LLC exempt from franchise fees in high-tax states such as California if it only holds vacant land in that state?

A case can be made that by passively holding vacant land an LP/LLC is not engaged in a trade or business and thus not subject to the state's franchise fees. Be sure to check with your local professional on this issue.

What happens if a Wyoming or Nevada LP or LLC holds rental real estate in an outside state?

Collecting rents on rental real estate is considered conducting a trade or business. The Wyoming or Nevada entity will have to qualify to do business and pay franchise fees in that state.

If I have rental real estate in an LP and take depreciation at the highest tax rate (35 percent at the time of this writing) what happens upon the sale of the property?

Pursuant to IRS §1250 you will have a recapture of depreciation at a 25 percent rate upon the sale of rental real estate.

Can LLCs be used for REITs (Real Estate Investment Trusts)?

Yes.

Is there ever a situation where not all members of an LLC are allocated recourse financing?

Yes. Where only one member personally guarantees the financing only that member – and not the others – will be allocated the recourse financing.

Chapter Ten
Joint Ventures and LLCs/LPs

The term "joint venture" is descended from the wild beginnings of capitalism. In the 1500s, as European nations and nationals were going to sea in search of opportunity and reward (or, as the politically correct would have it, to plunder, conquer and despoil), a new means of doing business was needed. To outfit and man a ship for a long ocean journey was usually too expensive for one investor. The operation required the financial assistance of many contributing investors.

And so, the single-purpose partnership was formed, which became more colorfully known as "the joint adventure." As discussed in more detail in my book, *Own Your Own Corporation*, eventually the corporate form of doing business, with its limited liability protection, became the preferred entity over general partnerships for such risky enterprises. But the term joint adventure, which was later commonly shortened to joint venture, resonated with the entrepreneurial class and has survived to describe the coming together of people and parties to pursue a common business objective.

With the recent advent of LLCs, joint ventures have found a new format for the pursuit of risk and reward.

<u>Case Number 8 - John and Kent; Chuck and Werner</u>

John and Kent are the owners of Cabeza, Inc., a think-tank involved in cutting edge research and development. Cabeza's strengths are in the creation and refinement of technologically advanced products, but they can never seem to take any of their developments to the marketplace. They have tried twice before and failed miserably. They are scientists, they sniff, not life insurance salesmen.

Chuck and Werner are the owners of Nah! Corporation. Nah! is all about the energy it takes to drive a product into the marketplace, establish a beachhead and spread out into the mainland, gaining converts and repeat business. Nah! sees the introduction of each product as the D-Day invasion. When they hit the beach at Normandy it is an all-out assault. If the scientists get in the way or can't keep up it's too darn bad. They have a market to capture.

Cabeza has developed a high-tech headset that allows a user to effortlessly perform five tasks at once. The patent application has been filed, the market needs the product, and John and Kent are stymied. They don't dare try marketing one of their own products again.

Then their lawyer introduces them to Chuck and Werner. The four seem to hit it off. Chuck and Werner have some immediate thoughts on how to market the product. Further discussions ensue and the two companies, through the four principals, decide to pursue a joint venture. Cabeza will be responsible for providing and continually updating the product. Nah! will be responsible for attacking the marketplace and selling huge quantities of product. It is agreed that it will be a 50/50 deal, with all parties active in the business and either sinking or swimming together.

But how to structure the joint venture? Their lawyer runs through the list of entity options:

1. C Corporation: The problem with a corporate joint venture is that to consolidate tax returns the Corporation must own 80 percent or more of the joint venture. Consolidating tax returns is important because it allows affiliated Corporations to net their earnings and losses for tax purposes. In this case neither joint venturer will own an 80 percent interest in the venture.
2. Sub-Chapter S Corporation: A Sub-Chapter S Corporation will not work because Cabeza and Nah! are both Corporations and thus ineligible shareholders for a Sub-Chapter S Corporation.
3. General Partnership: The original joint adventure format will not work because it provides no limited liability protection.
4. Limited Partnership: While a Limited Partnership provides limited liability protection, the management

and control issues are problematic. Since both Cabeza and Nah! want to be active in management and control of the business, a general partner will be needed, requiring control issues to be dealt with at both the general and Limited Partnership levels.

After reviewing four choices that are not ideal, the lawyer suggests using an LLC. He cites the following advantages:

1. The profits and losses from the LLC business can flow directly through to each Corporation. With an LLC there is no need to worry about holding an 80 percent interest for consolidating tax returns. In addition, with proper planning, certain income and losses can be specially allocated between the two Corporations if needed.
2. The Corporations are eligible to hold interests in an LLC, unlike with a Sub-Chapter S Corporation.
3. Unlike general or Limited Partnerships, the LLC provides limited liability protection while allowing for management and control to be shared by all parties.
4. As a member of an LLC, the joint venturer does not have any liability for the joint venture LLC's debts and obligations, unless it chooses to guarantee them.

The lawyer then discusses how management and control can be handled between the two companies. The joint venture LLC would be manager-managed, whereby each corporate member would be allowed to appoint two individuals to the managing board. The obvious choices were John and Kent from Cabeza and Chuck and Werner from Nah!

Then the issue of how to deal with a deadlock comes up. Since each Corporation has two representatives on the four-person board, the possibility of a tie on certain key issues is very real. The lawyer discusses several options with the four, including binding arbitration, submittal to an independent expert on the particular issue in dispute, or the appointment of a competent neutral manager to the board.

The four principals like the latter approach. They all agree it is helpful to have the view of an experienced person who does not hold any sort of interest in either joint venture partner or in the joint venture itself. The right person will be an objective observer and counselor and can be expected to break a tie vote in his or her independent judgment, in what he or she feels is the best interests of the joint venture, as opposed to the best interests of one joint venturer over another.

With that, the lawyer creates a manager-managed LLC. Each Corporation appoints two managers, and the four managers then select an independent fifth manager. The fifth manager is paid for each meeting attended.

To ensure the objectivity of the fifth manager, he or she is prohibited from: (1) holding any sort of interest in the joint venture or in either Corporation; and (2) receiving any sort of remuneration from either Corporation for any outside consulting or other services.

The LLC as managed by the five managers is able to operate smoothly and without rancor. By having to make a case to the independent manager that a proposed action is in the best interests of the joint venture, a calmer, clearer and more reasoned approach to decision-making is taken. Cabeza and Nah! both make a great deal of money.

Frequently Asked Questions

Can LLCs be used as joint venture vehicles in the medical field?

Yes, management service organizations, independent physician associations, physician-hospital organizations and other medical service ventures may use LLCs to their advantage. The LLC joint venture may be structured to preserve the independence of an individual practice while joining forces to be competitive in the managed-care marketplace. In addition, while some states prohibit certain professional groups from owning shares in another professional Corporation, there may be no such restriction on

LLC interests. However, if not-for-profit status is desirable, you must check with your state's law. Many states do not allow for non-profit LLCs.

Are LLCs subject to anti-trust laws?

Yes, as with corporate joint ventures, LLC joint ventures are subject to the anti-trust laws. You can't exert monopoly control with either a corporate or an LLC joint venture.

Can LLCs be used for international joint ventures?

Yes, in fact, LLCs may be a superior fit than other entities for such purposes. For a Sub-Chapter S Corporation, your foreign partners, if non-resident aliens or entities, cannot be shareholders. To achieve pass-through tax liability and limited liability protection, an LP or LLC may be used. But the LLC tends to match up better due to its similarity with many overseas business entities. In Germany, a Gesellschaft mit beschranker Haftung (GmbH) is very similar to (and the forefather of) the LLC. In France the Société a responsabilité limitée (SARL) and in South and Central America limitadas, both have the same characteristics of LLCs. Of course you must review each country's laws to understand the registration and tax requirements involved.

Can an LLC venture between a for-profit company and a non-profit company be formed?

Yes, although the IRS has certain very technical requirements that must be met, such an LLC joint venture can be formed.

How does the management work in a joint venture LLC?

The flexibility of management structure is an advantage for joint venture LLCs. Rather than be subject to the more rigid requirements of corporate structure, the partners can structure management to be in sync with the business dynamics of the joint venture itself.

Chapter Eleven
Intellectual Property and LLCs/LPs

Over the last twenty years, the importance of intellectual property has increased dramatically. The rights to patents and trademarks, copyrights and trade secrets may now be viewed as a company's most valuable asset.

At the very least, any halfway sophisticated purchaser of a business is going to want to know the status of the company's intellectual property. You can be certain that if your company has been using its very catchy, memorable and desirable name and slogans for some time, but has failed to obtain trademark protection on them, the value of your company will be reduced.

So, if intellectual property is so valuable, how do you hold it and protect it?

Case Number 9 - Theodore and Ryan

Theodore and Ryan have an idea for a terrific franchise opportunity. Theodore has developed patented exercise equipment that allows weary travelers to overcome the lethargy of jet lag. Ryan has obtained the trademark rights to "JetSweat" and has secured a lease at San Francisco International Airport (SFO) for the first airport health club/jet lag reduction center. Theodore and Ryan are very excited about JetSweat, Inc., and feel it can become a very successful franchise business.

Theodore and Ryan have consulted with an attorney about how to structure the transaction. They explain that they want the franchisor – the parent company – to be able to go public. Their attorney suggests that a Nevada C Corporation may be the best vehicle for that purpose.

Ryan is a California resident and he wants to have the California franchise rights to JetSweat, Inc. He will operate the first facility at SFO through this company. He knows that since he lives in California, any income either he or the

California business generates in California will be subject to California's fairly high personal and corporate income taxes. By creating a separate California entity with the franchise rights just for California, they can encapsulate all of the California tax obligations into one entity. The lawyer suggests that the California entity be a Sub-Chapter S Corporation. In this way, Ryan can obtain limited liability and flow-through taxation while avoiding California's unnecessarily high LLC fees. In addition, once Ryan receives a reasonable salary for his California efforts, any profits can flow through the Sub-Chapter S Corporation to him as profits, without the need to pay federal employment taxes.

It is decided then that other income generated around the world and outside California will be run through the Nevada parent company, thus allowing for California taxes to only be paid on California income. (Please note that California is just an example here. This concept applies to any high-tax state. Your strategy is to isolate high tax state taxes to only the income actually generated in the high-tax state. Any and all other revenues are generated through Nevada, or another no state tax jurisdiction such as Wyoming, thus reducing state tax obligations in the high-tax state.) The IRS is not upset by this strategy. Their corporate tax is paid no matter what state you do business in.

A key issue remains, and that is how to handle the intellectual property, the patent and the trademark. Theodore has obtained the patent in his name as is required. Inventors must apply for a patent as individuals. The patent may later be assigned to a Corporation, LLC or LP. While trademarks may be applied for in an entity's name, Ryan has applied for JetSweat, Inc., in his own name. The mark can be easily assigned to whatever entity he and Theodore decide to use.

The lawyer explains to them the advantages and disadvantages of holding the patent, trademark and any other future intellectual property obtained, such as copyrights and trade secrets, in an LLC. While an LP would also serve in this situation, for purposes of this discussion we shall use an LLC based in Wyoming.

The lawyer draws a chart of how the transaction will come together:

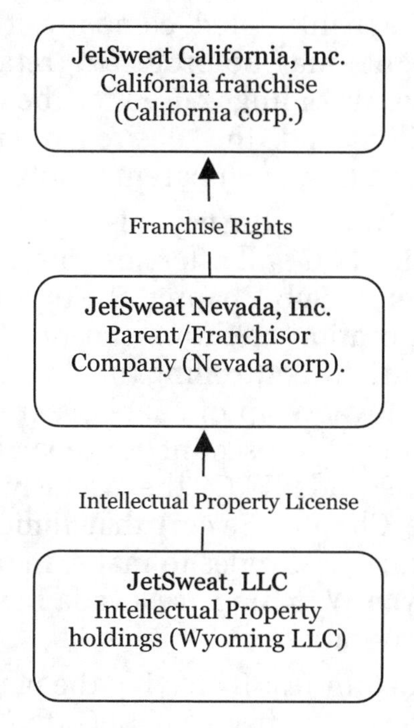

He then outlines the advantages and disadvantages of the intellectual property/LLC strategy as follows:

Advantages

1. Asset Protection: By holding the intellectual property in a Wyoming LLC separate from the Nevada parent Corporation (see chart), valuable assets are protected. If the parent were sued, the intellectual property, which is now licensed by the parent from a separate entity, is beyond the reach of creditors. Further, in certain high stakes intellectual property litigation, competitors may sue a company just to get a look at the patents and

trademarks. By licensing the intellectual property from an LLC, a barrier may be erected. In addition, assume the parent company has financial problems and files for bankruptcy. By holding the intellectual property outside of the bankrupted company, the patent and trademark rights may be protected, retained and used at a later time. Wyoming is used for the LLC because of its affordability and the desire to create distance between the entities, an apparent roadblock.

Theodore and Ryan's attorney also points out that a Wyoming (or Nevada) LLC will offer superior asset protection and advantages over a Sub-Chapter S Corporation. With a Sub-Chapter S Corporation creditors can reach shares of the company, thus potentially controlling the flow of the money to satisfy claims. With ownership of shares, a creditor can even sell the assets (usually at a discount) to repay him or herself. In a Wyoming or Nevada LLC, the exclusive remedy is a charging order (see Chapter Seven) that limits a creditor to distributions the manager decides to make. In order to protect intellectual property, a Wyoming or Nevada LLC is superior to a Sub-Chapter S Corporation.

2. Income Opportunities: By having the parent license the intellectual property from an LLC, the owners of the LLC may be able to generate a significant amount of flow-through income. Whether the LLC owners will be able to avoid the payment of federal employment taxes on such income is a question best answered with an accountant according to each specific fact pattern. Indeed, some accountants, from a pure tax standpoint, would rather use a Sub-Chapter S Corporation for this purpose. (Remember how a Sub-Chapter S Corporation can flow through monies without the payment of employment tax.) However, as mentioned, the asset protection benefits are superior with a Wyoming or Nevada LLC. Thus, it becomes a judgment call on the partners' part after weighing each entity's benefits.

Nevertheless, a Sub-Chapter S Corporation, an LLC or even an LP will allow license monies to flow from a Parent/Franchisor company, most likely a C Corporation, directly to the creative, worthy individuals who came up with the whole idea. That appeals to Theodore and Ryan.

Theodore is a Nevada resident, so all the flow-through monies (whether from Nevada or Wyoming, but not from California) come to him without the need to pay a state income tax. Ryan, a California resident, has to pay California state income tax on the flow-through monies he receives. But he likes the idea of using the Nevada and Wyoming entities because it helps Theodore, and it gives Ryan future flexibility, in that he is considering a future move to Nevada or perhaps Wyoming for tax and quality of life reasons.

3. <u>Control Opportunities</u>: In the event JetSweat Nevada, Inc., the parent/franchisor, goes public or receives venture capital funding, there is always the chance that Theodore and Ryan may lose control of the parent company. While in some cases losing control to a professional group of managers may increase a founder's share value, in other situations it may not be a beneficial or pleasant experience. By structuring the LLC intellectual property ownership strategy at the start, before any investment monies come in, Theodore and Ryan may gain leverage in any future control battles. As an example, the license agreement between the LLC and the parent company (which again, is best signed before any investors come in and is then fully disclosed to all investors) may give the LLC the right to cancel the contract and relicense the intellectual property to another party if certain conditions are not met. This is the kind of hammer that Theodore and Ryan may need in future negotiations. This strategy may also allow them to sell the LLC in tandem with the sale of the parent.

Disadvantages

1. State Tax Issues: Here is an interesting tax case involving an intellectual property strategy. (Please note that most tax cases are not at all interesting.)

Toys 'R Us, the world's largest retailer of children's toys, set up Geoffrey, Inc., to hold and license its trademarks. (Geoffrey, as you may know, is the Toys 'R Us giraffe and corporate mascot.) Geoffrey, Inc., a Delaware Corporation, received one percent of the net sales of products sold under the licensed marks. This is the same type of strategy we outlined in our JetSweat example.

As you might imagine, one percent of the net sales of Toys 'R Us is a significant amount of money. And what happens when large sums of money are identified?

States try to tax it.

The South Carolina Tax Commission saw a percentage of net sales being paid from the South Carolina Toys 'R Us stores to Geoffrey, Inc., pursuant to the license agreement. The effect was to reduce the taxable income of the South Carolina stores, thus reducing the Tax Commission's take. So the Tax Commission took a very bold stand and argued that Geoffrey, Inc., by licensing from Delaware into the state, was doing business in South Carolina and subject to state tax on the money it received from the South Carolina stores.

The Tax Commission stance was bold because Geoffrey, Inc. had no offices, employees or real or tangible property in South Carolina. As a general rule, if you're not present in a state, they can't tax you. So South Carolina's aggressive stance raised the big question:

> Does a state have the constitutional power to impose an income tax on a foreign Corporation with no physical presence in the state but whose intellectual property is being used in the state by a licensee?

Predictably, the South Carolina Supreme Court said yes (see 437 SE 2d, 13 (S.C. 1993)). Florida and Texas now also seek to tax such out-of-state revenues. But other states and a number of legal scholars have rejected the South Carolina decision. The taxation of an entity not physically present in the state is, for many, a clear violation of both the Due Process and Commerce Clauses of the United States Constitution, which require at least some minimum contacts for taxation.

We have not heard the end of this case.

Yet, for the purposes of this discussion, it is important to know that some states, whether rightly or wrongly, may seek to tax licensing revenues.

Theodore and Ryan are not deterred. If a state tries to come after them for taxes it just means they are making money, and that is a good thing.

2. No Investors: While there are several very good reasons to hold the intellectual property outside of the parent company, there is one very big reason why it may not fly. Investors want to invest in intellectual property. They like patents, trademarks, copyrights and trade secrets, which are considered to have value. They may not want to invest unless they own some of the good stuff.

In terms of strategy, by all means place the intellectual property into a separate LLC. Let the investors come with a term sheet stating that they'll put $10 million into the company only if the intellectual property is assigned to and owned by the company. The decision can then be made as to whether to proceed with this first group or wait until another investment group comes along that will allow the LLC to license valuable technology to the parent company. Or, if the first group's money is that important, assigning the LLC to the parent can be used as a bargaining chip to get higher salaries or other benefits. In all cases, the intellectual property/LLC strategy has merit and benefit. It certainly shows the investors that intellectual property has been well thought out and is highly valued.

If investors are not being sought, there are really no disadvantages to using the intellectual property/LLC or LP strategy. The minor costs of maintaining an additional entity (which in Wyoming is a $50 annual fee to the state and $125 for a resident agent each year) and preparing an extra tax return are more than offset by the asset protection, income and control opportunities gained by the strategy.

Frequently Asked Questions

Where can I learn more about patents, trademarks and other intellectual property matters?

For a good overview of the subject, read Michael Lechter's *Protecting Your #1 Asset: Creating Fortunes from your Ideas* (Warner Books, 2001). For more specific information on trademarking (as well as how to receive a free, 15-minute consultation with a trademark attorney), visit www.sutlaw.com.

Chapter Twelve
Admission, Withdrawal and Expulsion of Members/Partners

In most LLCs and LPs the issues of adding new members and partners and having existing members and partners withdraw or be expelled will come up. As the area is rule-driven we shall explore what the statutes say (and don't say) in this regard.

In many cases the best explanation is found by just reading the state statutes, and in such cases we will print and cite the statute number for your convenience. Please note that while a great many states have similar statutes (based on the Uniform Limited Partnership Act, for example) you should check your own state's codes to be certain that the general rules herein are applicable to your state.

In reviewing this subject we shall see that most states have default provisions in the event the Operating or Partnership Agreement do not provide direction. If the agreement is silent as to a certain issue, then by default the state statute applies. Accordingly, it is important to draft your agreement to cover the issues that are important to you.

Limited Partnerships

Admission of Additional General Partners

The rule in Nevada and certain other states is that:

> "After the filing of a limited partnership's original certificate of limited partnership, additional general partners may be admitted as provided in writing in the partnership agreement or, if the partnership agreement does not provide in writing for the admission of additional general partners, with the written consent of all partners." (NRS 88.445)

The written Partnership Agreement could override the code's default position of unanimous written consent by providing, for example, a majority consent of all partners.

Withdrawal or Expulsion of General Partners

As provided for in Nevada law (NRS 88.450 and 88.495) and those of several other states, except as otherwise approved by the unanimous written consent of all the partners, a person ceases to be a general partner through:

1. Written Notice of Withdrawal: "A general partner may withdraw from a limited partnership at any time by giving written notice to the other partners, but if the withdrawal violates the partnership agreement, the limited partnership may recover from the withdrawing general partner damages for breach of the partnership agreement and offset the damages against the amount otherwise distributable to him."

The key here is that if you are a general partner, make sure that your withdrawal is (1) acceptable under the Agreement and (2) won't damage the other partners. If your withdrawal causes an immediate dissolution, which then causes a $10 million land sale to fall apart causing the limiteds $9.5 million in lost profits, you may want to reconsider your withdrawal.

2. Assignment: When the general partner assigns his or her General Partnership interest to another, the new assignee does not automatically become the general partner but must be voted in by the limited partners.
3. Expulsion: The general partner can be expelled as a general pursuant to terms and conditions in the Partnership Agreement. This can be as a result of a majority (or higher percentage if you choose) vote of the limited partners. The expulsion can be for specific reasons or for no reason, just that the limiteds don't like the job the general partner is doing. The key point here is to make sure that what you want is clearly set out in your Limited Partnership Agreement.

4. Bankruptcy: If a general partner files for bankruptcy or is involuntarily placed in bankruptcy he or she is are automatically removed as a general partner, unless all the partners consent in writing to his or her continuance.
5. Death or Incompetence: When the general partner is not a Corporation or an LLC, but rather an individual, a death or a court determination of incompetence to manage affairs will constitute a withdrawal as a general partner.
6. Entity Termination. The dissolution of a Corporation, LLC or partnership as well as the termination of a Trust serving as a general partner is a withdrawal.

If a general partner leaves and other generals remain, under most state statutes the remaining generals may elect a new general partner to serve with them.

In the event a general partner withdraws and no one else remains as a general it is obviously important that a new general partner be voted in as soon as possible. The Partnership Agreement may provide that a majority or greater percentage vote of the limiteds shall be entitled to elect a new general partner. Nevertheless, when there is only one general partner and he or she withdraws, some courts may find that a dissolution has occurred, resulting in the need to liquidate or reconstitute the partnership. It is important that the Partnership Agreement be drafted to reflect the wishes of the organizers, which may be to continue the partnership by promptly voting in a new general partner.

It should be noted that when a general partner withdraws, he or she still remains personally liable for the debts and obligations incurred by the LP when he or she was general partner. This can be a significant burden. One can easily imagine a group of bad-hearted limiteds allowing the general to become obligated and then expelling him or her at a strategic point to their improper advantage. Again, this is just another example of why it makes sense to use a Corporation or LLC as a general partner.

Admission of Additional Limited Partners

Nevada law (NRS 88.420) and that of many other states provides that a person may be admitted as an additional limited partner upon:

1. Acquiring a Limited Partnership interest directly from the LP in compliance with the Partnership Agreement or, if the agreement is silent as to such a procedure, upon the written consent of all partners.
2. Assignment of a partnership interest from an existing limited in compliance with the Agreement or upon the consent of all partners.

Please note that if the assignor (the original limited partner transferring his or her interest) has not fully paid for his or her LP interest, he or she is are still responsible for that capital contribution even after the assignment of interest to a new limited partner.

Also note that the new limited partner is as responsible as the original limited partner for obligations to make and return contributions received from the LP when monies are later needed. As an example, Gimbal contributes $10,000 into Pressman Holdings, LP as a limited partner. Shortly thereafter he receives $5,000 of his contribution back. He then assigns his LP interest to Hagen, Moreira, Frank and Beck for $10,000 in accordance with the Partnership Agreement. The general partners, Duncan and Borden, now determine that the Limited Partnership needs the money back to pay creditors who extended credit when Gimbal's full $10,000 was held by Pressman Holdings, LP. For a set period of time (in Nevada it is one year if the contribution was properly returned, six years if improperly returned) Duncan and Borden can demand a return of the contribution. As such, not only Gimbal, but also Hagen, Moreira, Beck and Frank are individually each responsible for the $5,000 being paid back to Pressman Holdings, LP. The lesson is that if you are buying an LP interest be sure to do some due diligence (investigation) into what you are getting into.

Withdrawal or Expulsion of a Limited Partner

Absent a transfer of their LP interests, most limiteds do not withdraw. And because they are not involved in management (or at least are not supposed to be) they rarely are expelled. In the state of Washington and several other states, the law is as follows:

> "A limited partner may withdraw from a limited partnership at the time or upon the happening of events specified in and in accordance with the partnership agreement. If the partnership agreement does not specify the time or the events upon the happening of which a limited partner may withdraw, a limited partner may not withdraw prior to the time for the dissolution and winding up of the limited partnership." (RCW 825.10.330)

Which means as a limited you are stuck unless the Partnership Agreement gives you an out. So for what events could the agreement provide? Although not often seen in most Limited Partnership Agreements, provisions can be drafted allowing a limited partner to withdraw for:

1. Financial Reasons. For example, if annual contributions must be made and no one else will purchase the interest, the limited is allowed to withdraw. In such an instance the withdrawing limited could be held by the Agreement to have forfeited his or her interest and not be entitled to any distributions upon withdrawal.
2. Ethical or Moral Reasons. The agreement could provide that a limited may withdraw and forfeit his or her interest in objection to the LP's business decisions and objectives.

Certainly there could be other reasons providing for such a withdrawal. The point is that to allow for such events they must be specifically drafted for in the document. Absent a tailored Partnership Agreement most states' statutes do not allow limiteds to withdraw.

Distributions Upon Withdrawal

So a general or limited partner has withdrawn. How do you handle distributions?

First, remember that if the partner is transferring his or her interest to another individual or entity the company should not have to be concerned about distributions – that is, between the old and new partner. The scenario we have here is one where the partner has withdrawn without selling or transferring his or her interest to anyone else.

States have varying rules on the issue of how to compensate a withdrawing partner. For example, Nevada law, in part, states:

> "... [U]pon withdrawal any withdrawing partner is entitled to receive any distribution to which he is entitled under the partnership agreement and, if not otherwise provided in the agreement, he is entitled to receive, within a reasonable time after withdrawal, the fair value of his interest in the limited partnership as of the date of withdrawal based upon his right to share in distributions from the limited partnership." (NRS 88.505. See also, Ohio §1782.34)

On the other hand, Virginia law provides:

> "Except as otherwise provided in writing in the partnership agreement, neither a general partner nor a limited partner has any right to receive any distribution on account of (i) the partner's withdrawal or (ii) other event of dissolution or ceasing, for any other reason, to be partner." (Va Code § 50-73.39:1)

The key, once again, is to carefully draft the Partnership Agreement to reflect exactly how you want things handled. You may want to provide that the withdrawing partner is entitled to any distributions made to all partners prior to the date of the withdrawal and then a fixed or reduced amount for his or her partnership interest, to be paid when the partnership can afford to do so.

LLCs

Admission of New Members

Not all state statutes provide guidance as to how additional members are to be admitted. This is because such a procedure is usually provided for in the Operating Agreement.

A standard provision is to allow additional members to be admitted upon (1) payment for their interest (either from the company directly, or from an existing member), and (2) a vote of either or all or some majority percentage of the members. However, in the event you have neglected to provide an admission procedure in your Operating Agreement and your state's law is silent, you could look to Wisconsin's common-sense statute for guidance:

> "(1) In connection with the formation of a limited liability company, a person acquiring a limited liability company interest is admitted as a member of the limited liability company upon the later of the following to occur:
>
> (a) The formation of the limited liability company.
>
> (b) The time provided in and upon compliance with an operating agreement or, if the limited liability company does not have an operating agreement or an operating agreement does not so provide, on the effective date of the person's admission, as reflected in the records of the limited liability company ...
>
> (2) After the formation of a limited liability company, a person acquiring a limited liability

> company interest is admitted as a member of the limited liability company:
>
> (a) In the case of a person acquiring a limited liability company interest directly from the limited liability company, at the time provided in and upon compliance with an operating agreement or, if the limited liability company does not have an operating agreement or an operating agreement does not so provide, upon the consent of all members and on the effective date of the person's admission as reflected in the records of the limited liability company ...
>
> (b) In the case of an assignee of a limited liability company interest, ... at the time provided in and upon compliance with an operating agreement or, if the limited liability company does not have an operating agreement or an operating agreement does not so provide, on the effective date of the person's admission as reflected in the records of the limited liability company ..." (WI §183.0801)

Please note that the above-quoted statute is only legally binding for LLCs formed in Wisconsin. However, in situations where state law is silent as to an issue, courts will look to other state's statutes for guidance. The Wisconsin statute, which basically says that if you're listed in the company's records as a member, then you're a member, is a reasonable and prudent one to use in such a situation. The key, of course, is never to be in such a situation and instead specifically address the issue in your Operating Agreement.

Withdrawal or Expulsion of a Member

Again, member withdrawal and expulsion are issues to be specifically drafted into your Operating Agreement. You may want to allow withdrawal and expulsion or prohibit it. The choice is yours. But failure to do so will subject you to your state's statute. Such statutes differ greatly around the country.

Two state statutes are indicative of this variance. Nevada law provides:

> "Except as otherwise provided in chapter 463[3] of NRS, other applicable law, the articles of organization or the operating agreement, a member may not resign or withdraw as a member from a limited liability company before the dissolution and winding up of the company." (NRS 86.331, sub 1)

On the other hand, South Carolina's law provides for a greatly different outcome. (Feel free to skip forward, knowing that state laws differ.)

> "§ 33-44-601. Events Causing Member's Disassociation.
>
> A member is disassociated from a limited liability company upon the occurrence of any of the following events:
>
> (1) The company's having notice of the member's express will to withdraw upon the date of notice or on a later date specified by the member;
>
> (2) an event agreed to in the operating agreement as causing the member's disassociation;
>
> (3) upon transfer of all of a member's distributional interest, other than a transfer for security purposes or a court order charging the member's distributional interest which has not been foreclosed;
>
> (4) the member's expulsion pursuant to the operating agreement;
>
> (5) the member's expulsion by unanimous vote of the other members if:

---

[3] Please note that chapter 463 is the Nevada Gaming Control Act and an indication of how deeply the control of gaming runs through Nevada law.

(i) it is unlawful to carry on the company's business with the member;
(ii) there has been a transfer of substantially all of the member's distributional interest, other than a transfer for security purposes or a court order charging the members' distributional interest which has not been foreclosed;
(iii) within ninety days after the company notifies a corporate member that it will be expelled because it has filed a certificate of dissolution of the equivalent, its charter has been revoked, or its right to conduct business has been suspended by the jurisdiction of its incorporation, the member fails to obtain a revocation of the certificate of dissolution or a reinstatement of its charter or its right to conduct business; or
(iv) a partnership or a limited liability company that is a member has been dissolved and its business is being wound up.

(6) on application by the company or another member, the member's expulsion by judicial determination because the member:
(i) engaged in wrongful conduct that adversely and materially affected the business;
(ii) willfully or persistently committed a material breach of the operating agreement or of a duty owed to the company or the other members under section 33-44-409; or
(iii) engaged in conduct relating to the Company's business which makes it not reasonably practicable to carry on business with the member;

(7) the member's
(i) becoming a debtor in bankruptcy;

(ii) executing an assignment for the benefit of creditors;
(iii) seeking, consenting to, or acquiescing in the appointment of a trustee, receiver, or liquidator of the member or of all or substantially all of the member's property; or
(iv) failing, within ninety days after the appointment, to have vacated or stayed the appointment of a trustee, receiver, or liquidator of the member or of all or substantially all of the member's property obtained without the member's consent or acquiescence, or filing within ninety days after the expiration of a stay to have the appointment vacated;
(8) in the case of a member who is an individual:
(i) the member's death;
(ii) the appointment of a guardian or general conservator for the member; or
(iii) a judicial determination that the member has otherwise become incapable of performing the member's duties under the operating agreement;
(9) in the case of a member that is a trust or is acting as a member by virtue of being a trustee of a trust, distribution of the trust's entire rights to receive distributions from the company, but not merely by reason of the substitution of a successor trustee;
(10) in the case of a member that is an estate or is acting as a member by virtue of being a personal representative of an estate, distribution of the estate's entire rights to receive distributions from the Company, but not merely the substitution of a successor personal representative; or
(11) termination of the existence of a member if the member is not an individual, estate, or trust other

than a business trust." (SC, 1966 Act No. 343, §33-44-601

"§ 33-44-602. Member's power to dissociate; wrongful dissociation.

(a) Unless otherwise provided in the operating agreement, a member has the power to dissociate from a limited liability company at any time, rightfully or wrongfully, by express will pursuant to Section 33-44-601(1).

(b) If the operating agreement has not eliminated a member's power to dissociate, the member's dissociation from a limited liability company is wrongful only if:

(1) it is in breach of an express provision of the agreement; or

(2) before the expiration of the specified term of a term company:

(i) the member withdraws by express will;

(ii) the member is expelled by judicial determination under section 33-44-601(6);

(iii) the member is dissociated by becoming a debtor in bankruptcy; or

(iv) in the case of a member who is not an individual, trust other than a business trust, or estate, the member is expelled or otherwise dissociated because it willfully dissolved or terminated its existence.

(c) A member who wrongfully dissociates from a limited liability company is liable to the company and to the other members for damages caused by the dissociation. The liability is in addition to any other obligation of the member to the company or to the other members.

(d) If a limited liability company does not dissolve and wind up its business as a result of a member's wrongful dissociation under subsection (b), damages sustained by the company for the

> wrongful dissociation must be offset against distributions otherwise due the member after the dissociation."

Again, the issue remains: with a properly and thoroughly drafted Operating Agreement your state's statute most likely will not apply. Check your local rules and then draft an Operating Agreement that satisfies your own specific requirements.

Issues Involving Managers

It should also be noted that whereas we spoke of the addition and withdrawal of general partners in the LP context, the discussion for managers in the LLC context is more limited. There are two reasons. First, state laws are generally silent as to the issue. This is most likely due to the fact that LLCs are such new entities that state legislatures have not yet focused on the issue. Secondly, the admission and withdrawal of managers is an exclusive province of the Operating Agreement. It is the job of the original members to address the issue and provide their own procedures. Typically, additional managers are brought on by a majority or unanimous vote of all the members. Operating Agreements are also usually drafted to provide for their removal upon a majority or greater vote of the members. There is no set standard for withdrawal of a manager. A provision could be drafted allowing for a voluntary withdrawal but continuing liability (such as it may be) for all acts taken while manager. State law would impose this continuing liability anyway. Or, akin to the general partner scenario, a manager could withdraw by giving written notice to the other managers, but if withdrawing violated the Operating Agreement the LLC could seek damages and an offset against any distributions owed.

Distributions Upon Member Withdrawal

As always, the Operating Agreement controls the procedures in this area. How distributions are made is best determined by the founding members. Provisions to consider involve paying all distributions due prior to the withdrawal and then a fixed or reduced payment for their interest to be paid when the LLC can afford to acquire their interest.

In the event the Operating Agreement does not provide for such a procedure, it is again interesting to note how various states handle the issue. Nevada law provides:

> "Except as otherwise provided in this chapter, chapter 463 of the NRS, the articles of organization or the operating agreement:
>
> 1. If the resignation or withdrawal of a member violates the operating agreement:
>
> (a) the amount payable to the member who has resigned or withdrawn is the fair market value of his interest reduced by the amount of all damages sustained by the company or its other members as a result of the violation; and
>
> (b) the company may defer the payment for so long as necessary to prevent unreasonable hardship to the company.
>
> 2. Except as otherwise provided in chapter 463 of the NRS, the articles of organization or the operating agreement, a member who resigns or withdraws ceases to be a member, has no voting rights and has no right to participate in the management of the Company, even if under this section a payment due him from the company is deferred." (NRS 86.335)

With regard to distributions, and several other related matters, Tennessee law states:

> "(b) WHEN EXPULSION PERMITTED. Unless provided in the articles, a member may not be expelled.
>
> (c) EFFECT OF TERMINATION OF MEMBERSHIP ON THE GOVERNANCE RIGHTS OF THE TERMINATED MEMBER. If, for any reason, the continued membership of a member is terminated:

(1) If the existence and business of the LLC is continued, then the member whose membership has terminated loses all governance rights and will be considered merely an assignee of the financial rights owned before the termination of the membership; and

(2) Unless the articles or operating agreement provide otherwise, if the existence and business of the LLC is not continued, the member whose continued membership has terminated, except through wrongful withdrawal or wrongful termination, retains all governance rights owed before the termination of the membership and may exercise those rights through the winding up and termination of the LLC.

(d) ADDITIONAL EFFECTS IF TERMINATION OF MEMBERSHIP IS WRONGFUL. If a member withdraws in contravention of the articles or an operating agreement then:

(1) the member who has wrongfully withdrawn forfeits governance rights in the winding up and termination process or in the continued business; and

(2) the member who has wrongfully withdrawn is liable to all the other members and to the LLC to the extent damaged, including the loss of foregone profits, by the wrongful withdrawal. Such damages may be offset against any amount to be paid to the wrongfully withdrawing or terminating member by the LLC.

VALUE IF LLC IS CONTINUED. If the business and existence of the LLC are continued, any withdrawing or terminating member, whether such withdrawal or termination was wrongful or otherwise, is entitled to receive, subject to the provisions of subsection (d) above, the lesser of the fair market value of the withdrawing or terminating member's interest determined on a going concern basis or the fair market value of the withdrawing member's interest determined on a liquidation basis.

VALUE IF LLC TERMINATES. Except as provided in subsection (d), if the business and existence of the LLC are not continued, then any withdrawing or terminating member, whether such withdrawal or termination was wrongful or otherwise, is entitled to receive that member's distribution under § 48-245-1101.

TERMS OF PAYMENT. Except as provided in the articles or operating agreement, any amount to which a withdrawing or terminating member is entitled under subsection (e) or (f) shall be paid to such withdrawing or terminating member within six (6) months of the determination of such amount.

MODIFICATION BY ARTICLES OR OPERATING AGREEMENT. *Notwithstanding other provisions in this section*, the articles or operating agreement may establish the amount to be paid a withdrawing or terminating member or a method for establishing such amount and may also establish the terms of payment of such amount. Such established amount, or the method of determining such amount, and such established terms of payment shall control." (TN §48-216-101) (emphasis added)

The Tennessee law set out above makes clear the philosophy behind this entire chapter. Your state's law will, most times, defer to your entity's operating agreement. Your Operating Agreement controls how your LLC will operate. Your Partnership Agreement controls how your LP will operate. Think about what you want and write it into your Agreement.

Frequently Asked Questions

What happens to a general partner's interest when he or she withdraws or is expelled?

The Partnership Agreement should set out an approved scenario. In some cases, such as a buy-sell agreement, the general must sell his or her interest back to the partnership or the other partners. In others, the general is permitted to transfer his or her interest to a list of acceptable holders (another general partner, his or her heirs, other approved persons) who are then approved by a majority or greater vote of the generals and limiteds to hold the interest.

When does a partner cease to be a partner?

Nevada law states: "Except as provided in the partnership agreement, a partner ceases to be a partner upon assignment of all his partnership interest." (NRS 88.530) It is suggested that for the sake of certainty and sanity you may not want to draft a Partnership Agreement that keeps post-assignment partners involved. Once their interest is assigned they should be out as a partner. The same is true for a member in an LLC.

Chapter Thirteen
Transfers of Membership and Partnership Interests

Members or limiteds seeking to transfer or dispose of their interests must look first to the transfer or sale restrictions contained in the Operating Agreement or Partnership Agreement. For this reason it is important to draft the transfer/sale restrictions section carefully. If the intent of your LLC or LP is to operate as a closely held entity, where you have significant control over who may participate, then you do not want to leave the language vague, or say nothing at all, in which case state laws regarding transfers will apply by default.

Case Number 10 - Mark and Elizabeth

Mark and Elizabeth were real estate syndicators. Their business was to identify a piece of real estate in an appreciating area and acquire it with other investors, using an LLC or LP. They followed all the securities laws when bringing in investors and even put their own money into each project to show their other investors that they had confidence in the investment.

In many cases Mark and Elizabeth, for their management efforts and their cash contributions, would own 40 percent of the entity. Having been financially hurt in one real estate deal where the remaining 60 percent owners had sold their interest to the wrong group of people, they were careful on how transfers of interests took place. In the one bad deal, the 60 percent owners had transferred their interests to an aggressive group of individuals with reputed criminal back grounds. Without much thought, these people were admitted as full voting members. They immediately alleged that Mark and Elizabeth had breached their fiduciary duty to the business and sought to take away their 40 percent interest. At the same time Mark and Elizabeth began getting calls at 2:00 a.m.

warning them not to be stupid. They would awake to find the tires on their cars had been slashed.

It wasn't worth the stress. Mark and Elizabeth forfeited their 40 percent interest and moved on to future projects with better partners.

But they learned their lesson. They would not allow a transfer of an interest without unanimous consent of all partners/members. This requirement was written into every new Operating Agreement and Partnership Agreement they used. In this way, if they did not like the new people, or if a background check turned up negative information, they could vote to not grant incoming individuals full partner/member status. And while such a move may not fully protect them from the pit bulls of criminal enterprise, it did serve to protect them from the lesser breeds of aggressive and mean-spirited investors.

Mark and Elizabeth also included a Buy-Sell provision in their documents. This procedure required members or limiteds to first offer their interest to the other members or limiteds for a set period of time (say, 30 days). If no other members or limiteds came forward to purchase the member or partnership interest, then the offer to purchase must be made to the LLC or LP itself, allowing another set period of time for it to repurchase the member's interest. If the LLC or LP also declines to purchase the interest, then the transfer proceeds. However, the Operating or Partnership Agreement was also be drafted to prevent the transferee (person or entity receiving the interest) from actually becoming a member or a limited. The transferee may hold the interest representing an economic value, but may not participate in the operation of the LLC or LP, have no voting rights, and is, for all intents and purposes, a passive interest holder. Such holder is often referred to as an "assignee." The members or limiteds may subsequently vote to allow an assignee to become a member or limited, but in Mark and Elizabeth's documents this required the unanimous written consent of all members/partners..

It is important to know what will happen if you don't provide for such a transfer procedure. Generally your state's LLC or LP statute will have a default provision that will apply. Nevada law on this matter is indicative:

Limited Partnership

> "Except as provided in the partnership agreement, a partnership interest is assignable in whole or in part. An assignment of a partnership interest does not dissolve a limited partnership or entitle the assignee to become or to exercise any rights of a partner. An assignment entitles the assignee to receive, to the extent assigned, only the distribution to which the assignor would be entitled. Except as provided in the partnership agreement, a partner ceases to be a partner upon assignment of all his partnership interest." (NRS 88.530)
>
> ***
>
> "1. An assignee of a partnership interest, including an assignee of a general partner may become a limited partner if and to the extent that:
>
> (a) the assignor gives the assignee that right in accordance with authority described in the partnership agreement; or
>
> (b) All other partners consent.
>
> 2. An assignee who has become a limited partner has, to the extent assigned, the rights and powers, and is subject to the restrictions and liabilities, of a limited partner under the partnership agreement and this chapter. An assignee who becomes a limited partner also is liable for the obligations of his assignor to make and return contributions as provided in NRS 88.490 to 88.525, inclusive. However, the assignee is not obligated for

liabilities unknown to the assignee at the time he became a limited partner.
3. If an assignee of a partnership interest becomes a limited partner, the assignor is not released from his liability to the limited partnership under NRS 88.385 and 88.475." (NRS 88.540)

Limited Liability Company

"1. The interest of each member of a limited liability company is personal property and the articles of organization or operating agreement may prohibit or regulate the transfer of a member's interest. Unless otherwise provided in the articles or agreement, a transferee of a member's interest has no right to participate in the management of the business and affairs of the company or to become a member unless a majority in interest of the other members approve the transfer. If so approved, the transferee becomes a substituted member. The transfer is only entitled to receive the share of profits or other compensation by way of income, and the return of contributions, to which his transferor would otherwise be entitled.
2. A substituted member has all the rights and powers and is subject to all the restrictions and liabilities of his transferor except that the substitution of the transferee does not release the transferor from any liability to the company." (NRS 86.351)

It is important to note that in both cases the transferor (selling party) remains responsible for any liabilities to the company. If liabilities are an issue, a selling party may want to have a written agreement signed whereby the buying party or the remaining members/partners indemnify (agree to be responsible) for any liabilities. At the very least, a seller should not think that by merely transferring interest he or she can escape liability for obligations and responsibilities incurred while he or she was a member/partner.

Frequently Asked Questions

As you discuss in the next chapter, the free transferability of interests is a corporate characteristic and to be avoided for IRS purposes. Does the IRS require a unanimous vote for transfer consent?

No. The IRS allows a majority interest consent procedure for the transfer of interests.

Does the IRS require the transfer consent to be in writing?

Not at this time. But the better practice is to have all or a majority of the partners/members consent to the transfer and issue new interest certificates reflecting the transfer.

Do any states prohibit the transfer of a member/partner interest?

No. While transferees may become assignees and not full, substituted members/partners unless voted upon, there is no state prohibition on transfers to assignees. Remember though that buy-sell provisions may prolong the process of a transfer to an assignee.

What rights does an assignee have?

Generally, most states limit an assignee to an economic interest with financial rights but no voting rights.

What fiduciary duties does the majority owe to the minority, especially non-member assignees, in an LLC?

The law is not well-developed with regard to LLCs on this issue. In an LP context, general partners owe their limiteds a fiduciary duty of care without regard to ownership percentages. But the duties owed by majority members to minority members in an LLC is not yet clearly defined. Some states, however, allow for managers/general partners to have very few duties to assignees.

Is there a difference between transfers to existing members/partners and transfers to non-members/partners?

Some states do make the distinction in their statutes, requiring a consent procedure only for transfers to non-members/partners. The IRS, for its purposes, requires only that the consent procedure be applied to non-members/partners. You should check your state's statute to ascertain what is required. And remember, if voting rights and control issues are a concern, you may want to require a consent procedure in all cases.

Do the securities laws apply to transfers of interests?

Yes. See Chapter Five for a discussion of these issues.

Chapter Fourteen
Entity Dissolution

The word "dissolution" is deceptive in the context of partnership law. It does not mean termination of the business. Dissolution is a step before any winding up of the entity's business. It is more like a wake up call that some decisions must be made. So when a dissolution occurs, in most cases, the parties have two choices:

1. Agree to terminate the business; or
2. Agree to continue the business.

What are the events of dissolution that can bring about the need for this decision? In brief, in both partnerships and LLCs, a dissolution can arise:

1. By agreement, usually unanimous, of the parties in interest.
2. By an act of the parties.
3. By operation of law; or
4. By court order.

Please note that if the entire concept of dissolution seems unnecessarily awkward and formal – and perhaps even nonsensical – to you, you are in good company. The whole notion is a result of trying to cut and fit square pegs into square holes so as to achieve partnership taxation.

Some background information is helpful. Previously, when deciding how to tax entities, the IRS looked at four corporate characteristics:

1. Continuity of life.
2. Free transferability of interest.
3. Centralized management; or
4. Limited liability.

If three characteristics were present, the entity was taxed as a Corporation. If two of the four characteristics were lacking, an entity – be it an LLC or partnership – was classified as a partnership for federal income tax purposes.

Thus, in order to obtain flow-through taxation, certain gyrations had to occur to ensure that two characteristics were lacking. One way states assisted their citizens in this regard was to statutorily create the fiction of a dissolution, which showed that there was no continuity of life in partnerships and LLCs. If someone left, the whole thing came apart and dissolved – unless the others agreed to continue. Well, of course the partners are going to continue, unless they want to terminate the business. But they can terminate whenever they want to – with or without a dissolution event. So why interpose a dissolution, which can only create legal jeopardy for some and increased professional fees for others? Because the charade was needed to satisfy the IRS.

The second corporate characteristic the states sought to limit was the transferability of interests. Unlike corporate shares, the free transferability of partnership interests had to be statutorily restricted which, as we have seen, is a beneficial feature of these entities. With the elements of continuity of life and transferability of interests choked off under state law, flow-through taxation could be achieved. But now, with the IRS's enlightenment in allowing partnerships to elect to be taxed as Corporations and Sub-Chapter S Corporations to be taxed like partnerships, there is no need for the silly fiction of a dissolution. One can hope that states will see the light and amend their laws.

But because dissolution is still an LLC or LP feature, we'll use our next case to review certain dissolution scenarios. While an LLC is used in the example, the same is applicable to an LP.

Case Number 11 – Scott and Megan

Scott and Megan are dentists with a thriving practice. On their accountant's advice they have formed and used an LLC for conducting their business.

Scenario 1

Scott and Megan filed the Articles of Organization for S & M Dentistry, LLC with their state over five years ago when their state law (and many other state's law as well) required that LLCs exist only for a limited period not to exceed 30 years (again, a continuity of life charade). While their state's law has been changed to allow for perpetual duration, Scott and Megan have failed to amend their Articles of Organization, which uniquely only provide for a five-year term.

By the act of the parties, S & M Dentistry, LLC will dissolve on the date set forth in the articles as the last date of existence of the LLC. Depending on their state law, Scott and Megan may be able to amend their Articles by mutual agreement and continue the business. Or they may have to wind up and terminate the first LLC and then form a second LLC to continue their practice.

Scenario 2

Megan finds that she wants to spend more time with her children. She has earned enough money to retire and doesn't want to miss seeing them grow up. Scott agrees with Megan that Martin, an experienced dentist with many years of service in several dental practices, can take her place as a partner/member.

The retirement of one partner and the admission of a new partner is a dissolution event. In many states the following are dissolution events:

1. Bankruptcy of a party.
2. Death of a party.
3. Retirement or resignation of a party.
4. Expulsion of a party.
5. Insanity or other incompetence of a member.

As we discussed previously, it should be noted that while some states allow for the voluntary withdrawal of member(s)/partner(s), others actually prohibit such a withdrawal unless it is provided for in the operating or Partnership Agreement. Scott, Megan and Martin may have to sign paperwork unanimously agreeing to continue the LLC with just Scott and Martin.

Scenario 3

Scott and Martin form a new agreement to replace the one dissolved by Megan's retirement. After six months Scott learns why Martin has been associated with so many dental practices. Martin is dishonest, habitually drunk and abandons his obligations to the business. Because Martin owns 50 percent of the company, Scott cannot unilaterally fire him.

Scott's solution is to obtain a court order dissolving the LLC. By operation of law, a partnership or LLC can be dissolved for the misconduct or incapacity of a partner as well as for a breach of the partnership or Operating Agreement.

Upon the occurrence of a dissolution event the entity automatically dissolves, unless the remaining members vote to continue the business. While many states used to require the unanimous consent of the remaining members to continue, the general rule now is that unanimity is not required if a lesser amount is set out in the filing or organizational documents.

Scott obtains the court order he needs in short order. Four years previously, Martin had botched a root canal on the judge's son. The judge refuses to recuse himself and grants Scott all he wants.

Scott promptly files articles of dissolution with the secretary of state's office and follows his state's procedure for notifying the LLC's creditors.

Scott then proceeds to liquidate the LLC. As mentioned, a dissolution event calls into question whether to liquidate and wind up the business or not. If the answer is yes, and in Scott's case it is an emphatic yes, the process of liquidation begins. This involves discontinuing all of the LLC or partnership's business and distributing the assets first to creditors and then, if anything is left, to members.

There are two further issues to note in our dissolution discussion: state laws and unexpected tax termination.

State Laws

It is important to know your own state's law with regard to dissolution. The rules vary from state to state. Consider this LLC law in South Dakota:

> "A member of a limited liability company may have the limited liability company dissolved and its affairs wound up if:
> (1) The member rightfully but unsuccessfully has demanded the return of his contribution; or
> (2) The other liabilities of the limited liability company have not been paid, or the limited liability company property is insufficient for their payment and the member would otherwise be entitled to the return of his contribution." (South Dakota §47-34-30)

The consequences of this law are dramatic. Any time a member wants his money back he can demand it. If he doesn't get it, he can have the company wound up. There is not much comfort in being a manager of a South Dakota LLC. You certainly wouldn't want to invest in real estate or some other less-than-liquid investment when someone owning one percent of the deal who needs cash for a kitchen remodel can demand his or her money back. And if you don't give the money to him or her, he or she can force the LLC to sell its assets (usually at a discount) and thoroughly disrupt everyone else's investment.

The point here is that each state has different laws. Be sure you or your advisors are comfortable with the law of your land.

Unexpected Tax Termination

It is important to know that for tax purposes an LP or LLC can be unexpectedly terminated if within a twelve-month period there is a sale or exchange of 50 percent or more of the total interest in partnership or membership capital and profits.

When a termination based upon a sale or exchange occurs, the LP or LLC is deemed to have distributed its assets to the purchaser and remaining members in proportion to their respective interests in the entity. Immediately following this distribution, the purchaser and remaining members are treated as having contributed the assets to a new LP or LLC, which is actually the existing entity. The members can then decide whether to continue or dissolve.

While all this appears to be a legal fiction and a nuisance – it is both – there can be consequences to such an unexpected termination. Although generally a nontaxable event, a tax termination may force the remaining members to recognize a gain or loss. In addition, all old tax elections terminate and new ones must be made. Certainly, some have deliberately triggered a tax termination so as to reorder their entity. However, before you engage in such a strategy, and before you sell or exchange 50 percent or more of interests in one year, consult with your tax professional.

It should be noted here that a Sub-Chapter S Corporation may also have its tax election unexpectedly terminated. A Sub-Chapter S Corporation ceases to receive flow through taxation treatment if:

1. It has more than 75 shareholders.
2. A nonresident alien becomes a shareholder.
3. It has more than one class of stock or becomes a member of an affiliated group.
4. It acquires a subsidiary Corporation.

The consequences of losing your Sub-Chapter S status are significant. You may not reelect Sub-Chapter S status for a period of five years following the termination, although the

IRS does have a procedure to unwind innocent and inadvertent Sub-Chapter S Corporation terminations.

In all cases involving LPs, LLCs and Sub-Chapter S Corporations, an unexpected tax termination can range from a nuisance to a major problem. The most difficult part may be explaining to your investors and partners that you unexpectedly lost your flow-through tax status. Care should be taken to know and follow the rules in order to avoid such surprises.

Frequently Asked Questions

What is the difference between a dissolution and a liquidation?

A dissolution is a technical termination, which may lead to a continuance of the entity or a liquidation of the entity. A liquidation involves discontinuing the business and distributing assets to creditors and/or member(s)/partner(s).

Following a dissolution event, how much time do parties have to decide whether to continue the business or not?

Most states require a decision on whether or not to continue a business within 90 days of a dissolution event.

What rights do the remaining member(s)/partner(s) have after the dissolution event of another member/partner?

The remaining member(s)/partner(s) may continue the business, in which case the LLC/LP is not dissolved.

What happens if the remaining member(s)/partner(s) do not continue the business?

If it is decided that the business will not continue, the LLC/LPs business is liquidated and wound up.

How is an entity liquidated and wound up?

The assets are sold and distributions are made according to an order of priority. Some states will require an accounting of the entity's assets and liabilities to be prepared.

Who has the authority to windup a partnership or LLC?

The organizational documents should designate who shall be responsible for winding up a partnership or LLC and whether compensation is to be paid. If the document is silent as to authority to wind up, state statutes generally give such powers to the managers and then the members, or to the general partners and then, if no general partners remain, the limited partners. Some state statutes will provide that one who wrongfully dissolved the entity shall have no authority in winding it up. In some cases, a court-appointed trustee may wind up the entity.

Must anyone be notified of a dissolution or liquidation?

If a dissolution event occurs but the parties decide to continue with business no disclosure is necessary. In the event of a liquidation a number of states require creditors be notified.

What is the order of priority for the distribution of assets upon the winding up of an LLC/LP?

Generally, most states provide for accounts to be settled first to pay creditors, then to pay members/partners owed their distributions, then to pay members/partners a return of their capital contributions and finally, if any money is left, to pay according to members/partners percentage of ownership.

What if there is not enough money left to pay off the creditors?

Generally, additional contributions from members/partners will not be required to satisfy creditor claims. However, if an interest holder has not yet paid in their capital contribution or if improper distributions were received, a member/partner could be forced to pay in amounts owed.

What information must be contained in articles of dissolution filed with the state?

While each state's requirements differ, generally the following information must be set forth:

LLC: A declaration or statement, signed by the manager(s) that the LLC has (1) paid, discharged or made adequate provision to pay all of its liabilities, debts and obligations, (2) distributed all remaining assets among the members and (3) there are no lawsuits pending against the LLC, or adequate provision has been made to pay any claims which are in process.

LP: A declaration or statement, signed by all general partner(s) confirming the name and original formation date of the LP, as well as providing a reason for the dissolution.

What are the tax consequences of a dissolution?

It depends if the business continues or not. If it continues with two members/partners, there are no real consequences and the entity will continue to be taxed as a partnership. If the business ceases operations and liquidates there may be gains or losses attributable to the members/partners.

With an unexpected tax termination, must the entity obtain a new employer ID number from the IRS?

No, you don't need a new EIN. The entity created will retain its existing EIN number.

Chapter Fifteen
How and When Not to Use an LLC/LP

As important as knowing how and when to use an LLC/LP is knowing how and when not to use one.

Up until now, we have been discussing how the strategic use of business entities can help you to protect assets and conduct family wealth transfers. However, the same reasons that make Corporations, LLCs and LPs attractive for legitimate reasons also make them attractive for other purposes, some of which are illegal in most states.

There are three major areas of concern associated with the transfer of assets. They are fraudulent conveyances, Medicare fraud and money laundering. Because you do not want to be associated with any of them we shall review each one:

<u>Fraudulent Conveyance</u>: A fraudulent conveyance is a transfer of assets made intentionally, or found to be intentional, in an attempt to avoid creditors or judgments. If you know that you are likely to be sued in the near future, or if you have been served with legal proceedings, you may not form a business entity and transfer all of your personal assets into it in an attempt to avoid a possible judgment.

For example, let's assume that you own a four-plex in your own name. There is a staircase at the back of the property, which is getting old, is a bit rickety and is on your list of things to replace. Unfortunately, before you replace it, one of your tenants falls down the staircase and is injured when the handrail breaks. The tenant retains an attorney and you receive a letter notifying you that the tenant is claiming damages against you for his injuries. You had been meaning to transfer the four-plex into the name of your LLC and decide that now would be a good time, considering if this tenant sues you, you could risk a judgment attaching to the four-plex. Unfortunately, the matter does not settle, and when it goes to trial, the tenant's attorney makes a claim that you fraudulently conveyed the four-plex into the name of the LLC in an attempt to protect it from a valid claim. In addition to finding you at fault for the tenant's injuries, the court also rules that by transferring the four-plex into the name of the LLC after you had been notified of the tenant's claim, you have committed a fraudulent conveyance. The court rules that the four-plex must be transferred back into your name, and the tenant allowed to attach his judgment against it. The court also fines you for your attempt to avoid the judgment by conducting the transfer in the first place.

Most states have passed the Uniform Fraudulent Transfer Act (UFTA). Under the UFTA, the term "creditor" means simply a "person who has a claim," even if that claim is disputed and not yet reduced to judgment. If the court determines that a transfer was made with the intent to hinder, delay or defraud a creditor, the transfer is subject to a number of legal challenges. The law requires the court to consider a variety of factors, some of which indicate the absence of fraudulent intent. These factors include whether:

- The transfer was to an insider (which includes a relative, a Corporation in which the debtor is an officer, director, or a person in control or a partnership in which the debtor is a general partner or an affiliate)
- The debtor retained possession or control over the property transferred
- The transfer was disclosed or concealed
- The transfer included a substantial amount of the debtor's assets ("substantial" is a relative term and for the courts to decide
- The debtor absconded
- The debtor removed or concealed assets
- The debtor received reasonably equivalent value as consideration for the transfer
- The transfer rendered the debtor insolvent
- The debt occurred shortly before or shortly after a substantial debt was incurred

- The debtor transferred the essential asset of a business to a lienor who then transferred the assets to an insider

A creditor who proves that a transfer was made with the requisite intent to hinder, delay or defraud the creditor can request the court to void the transfer, enjoin future transfers, appoint a receiver and/or satisfy the claim out of the transferred property.

How do you avoid a fraudulent conveyance issue? By setting up your asset protection structures long before you ever get sued. For example, if the owners of the four-plex had transferred it into the LLC when they first bought the property, a tenant who started renting a year later could not say the structure was fraudulent. There was no intent to defraud the tenant – the owners did not even know the tenant when the LLC structure was implemented.

The rule of thumb is to set up your asset protection when the seas are calm. When there is clear sailing and no troubles ahead, you are perfectly within your rights to structure your affairs to your advantage. When the seas get rough, either your assets have been previously protected or they have not. At that point it is too late for transfers.

Medicare Fraud: Medicare fraud occurs when individuals transfer assets into the name of an entity in order to reduce their personal income or conceal their assets to pass income and net worth tests for Medicare eligibility.

For example, say your parents are retired and living on a small, fixed pension. They also hold several real estate properties, which have a combined value of $1.5 million. Your father's health is failing, however, and your mother is anticipating that his medical expenses are about to increase dramatically. Although your parents live on a fixed pension and qualify for Medicare benefits on that basis, by adding in the value of their real estate holdings, they become ineligible. Your mother is wondering how she will keep up your father's medical expenses on their pension, and is anticipating having to sell at least one of the properties to make sure there is enough money to cover them. You feel that if your parents formed a Limited Partnership with a corporate general partner, and transferred all of their real estate holdings into the Limited Partnership, the assets would no longer be in their name. Without having the assets in their name, they could then report their pension income on their Medicare application and qualify for benefits.

This type of transaction is considered fraudulent and is prohibited. Medicare fraud is a federal offense, which can result in severe monetary penalties. For more information, the Health Care Financing Administration, which administers Medicare, Medicaid and state Children Health Insurance programs, maintains a Web site at www.hcfa.gov.

Please bear in mind, however, that there is a difference between Medicare fraud and proper estate planning. Estate planning is a strategy to minimize the tax burden on your estate, and to ensure that you are able to transfer a maximum amount of wealth to your heirs with a minimum tax payment to the federal and state governments. The best way to avoid a possible claim of Medicare fraud is to make sure that estate planning begins early, and while everyone is in good health.

Money Laundering. Money laundering occurs when the proceeds of crime are funneled through a business entity in order to create the appearance of legitimate income. For example, a drug ring forms an LLC to purchase real estate properties. The members use a regular Corporation as the manager of the LLC, and use the proceeds from sales of drugs to purchase their membership interests in the LLC. The LLC then takes the money received from its members and purchases luxury real estate on Martha's Vineyard.

This is money laundering, which is a criminal offense at both state and federal levels. Parties convicted of money laundering can face jail, monetary penalties and the seizure and sale of assets bought with the proceeds of crime.

The Money Laundering Control Act (MLCA) makes it criminal for anyone to conduct or attempt to conduct certain financial activities that involve the proceeds of unlawful activities. The transfer of assets into a Corporation, Limited

Partnership, Trust or other entity can constitute a financial activity within the scope of the MLCA. The specified unlawful activities under the MLCA consist primarily of drug trafficking offenses, financial misconduct and environmental crimes.

Drug trafficking offenses include the manufacture, importation, sale or distribution of controlled substances; the commission of acts constituting a continuing criminal enterprise; and the transportation of drug paraphernalia.

Covered financial misconduct includes the concealment of assets from a receiver, custodian, trustee, marshal or other officer of the court, from creditors in a bankruptcy proceeding, or from the Federal Deposit Insurance Corporation, the Resolution Trust Corporation, or a similar agency or person; the making of a fraudulent conveyance in contemplation of a bankruptcy proceeding; bribery; the giving of commissions or gifts for the procurement of loans; theft, embezzlement, or misapplication of bank funds or funds of fraudulent bank or credit institution entries or loan or credit applications; and mail, wire, or bank fraud or bank or postal robbery or theft.

Environmental crimes include violations of the Federal Water Pollution Control Act, the Ocean Dumping Act, the Safe Drinking Water Act, the Resources Conservation and Recovery Act and similar federal statutes.

Other specified crimes include counterfeiting, espionage, kidnapping, or hostage taking, copyright infringement, entry of goods by means of false statements, smuggling of goods into the United States, removing goods from the custody of Customs, illegally exporting arms and trading with United States enemies.

So by engaging in these activities and then transferring the proceeds into another entity, you have compounded the claims against you.

How do you avoid a money laundering issue? Simple: don't do it. There is too much money to be made in this world by engaging in legal activities. You really do not need the sleepless nights of criminal enterprise.

Frequently Asked Questions

My estranged husband gets served with divorce papers. A week later he transfers a major asset out of our Limited Partnership to a Corporation he controls. Is that a fraudulent conveyance?

This is absolutely a fraudulent conveyance. Subject to each state's law, your attorney should immediately petition the court to void the transfer.

My reading of the Money Laundering Control Act is that it is very broad. What are the pitfalls?

The Money Laundering Control Act is an extremely broad piece of legislation designed as a catchall for all sorts of crimes and offenses. In practice, it is used even more broadly by federal prosecutors to gain leverage over those they have charged. For this reason, you must be very careful about wiring money in and out of the United States. A small or even innocent infraction can blossom into a full-scale money laundering charge as the law is being currently applied.

Chapter Sixteen
Entity Conversion

Because into every life a little uncertainty must fall, it stands to reason that as your business develops and becomes more complex, there may come a point where your carefully planned and structured business entity no longer fits your business needs. In order to keep moving forward, you will have to make some changes. For example, you may wish to convert an LLC into a C Corporation, or vice versa, or you may decide that your Limited Partnership would be more effective if it were organized as an LLC. Alternatively, you may decide that the tax advantages to a Nevada business entity outweigh the lower costs in your home state, and you would like to re-register your business entity as a Nevada business entity. This chapter will deal with the methods of various conversion types, and any resulting tax or other consequences.

Domestication of a Foreign Business Entity into a Nevada Entity

Nevada law has changed to allow a foreign (non-Nevada) business entity to register to become a Nevada business entity. (For a unique advantage the State of Wyoming offers, see the last question at the end of this chapter). The steps to domesticate a foreign entity into the same type of Nevada entity are as follows:

Step 1: The foreign entity must determine if the transfer to Nevada jurisdiction is permitted under the laws of its jurisdiction of incorporation.

Step 2 The shareholders or limited partners or members must prepare written Articles of Domestication, which sets out the following information:

1. Date of incorporation or organization of the foreign entity, as well as the jurisdiction of incorporation or organization.

2. Name of the foreign entity.
3. Name and type of entity the foreign entity intends to domesticate into.
4. Current jurisdiction of incorporation or organization.

Step 3: In addition to the Articles of Domestication, the foreign entity must also prepare the appropriate constituent document for the new entity: either Articles of Incorporation, Articles of Organization or a Certificate of Limited Partnership, depending on the entity being domesticated.

Step 4: The foreign entity must appoint a resident agent within Nevada and prepare a Certificate of Acceptance of Appointment as Resident Agent.

Step 5: The shareholders, limited partners or members must hold a general meeting, at which the Articles of Domestication must be approved by either a unanimous vote or the required majority under the foreign entity's bylaws, Limited Partnership Agreement or Operating Agreement.

Step 6: Following receipt of shareholder, limited partner or membership approval, the foreign entity must file the following documents and appropriate filing fees with the Nevada Secretary of State:

- Articles of Domestication
- Articles of Incorporation, Articles of Organization or Certificate of Limited Partnership, as appropriate
- Certificate of Acceptance of Appointment as Resident Agent
- The required filing fee of $350.00

Conversion from one form of Nevada Business Entity to Another

Nevada has also enacted new legislation setting out how Nevada business entities may be converted into other Nevada business entities.

The process to convert a Nevada entity is relatively straightforward. The entity to be converted must take the following steps:

Step 1: The shareholders, limited partners or members must prepare a written Plan of Conversion, which sets out the following information:

- The name and address of the existing entity and the name and address of the proposed new entity
- The jurisdiction of the existing and new entity
- The terms and conditions of the conversion
- The manner and calculations by which the shares or Limited Partnership interests or membership interests in the existing entity will be converted into shares, Limited Partnership interests or membership interests in the new entity
- The full text of the new entity's constituent documents (for a Corporation, this would be the Articles of Incorporation and bylaws, for a Limited Partnership it would be the Certificate of Limited Partnership and Limited Partnership Agreement, and for an LLC, it would be the Articles of Organization and the Operating Agreement)
- Any other provisions required by the existing entity

Step 2: The shareholders, limited partners or members must hold a general meeting, at which the Plan of Conversion must be approved by either a unanimous vote or the required majority under the existing entity's bylaws, Limited Partnership Agreement or Operating Agreement.

Step 3: The new entity must appoint a resident agent within Nevada.

Step 4: Following receipt of shareholder, limited partner or membership approval, the existing entity must prepare and file the following documents and appropriate filing fees with the Nevada Secretary of State:

- Articles of Conversion, which set out the names and jurisdiction of organization of both the existing entity and the new entity. The Articles of Conversion must also contain a statement by the existing entity that a Plan of Conversion has been prepared in accordance with Nevada law and has been approved by the shareholders, limited partners or members, as required; and

- Where the new entity is a:
  - Corporation, the new Articles of Incorporation; or
  - Limited Partnership, the new Certificate of Limited Partnership; or
  - LLC, the new Articles of Organization; and
- A Certificate of Acceptance of Appointment as Resident Agent; and
- The required filing fee of $350.00 to file the Articles of Conversion

Domestication and Simultaneous Conversion of Foreign Business Entity

It is also possible under the new Nevada legislation to do both a domestication and conversion simultaneously. Foreign entities wishing to conduct a conversion must first determine whether the conversion and domestication is permitted under existing law, and then follow the steps set out for a regular Nevada entity conversion. The same filing fee of $350.00 will be required for the simultaneous domestication and conversion.

Effect of Domestication

Once the documents have been filed and accepted by the secretary of state, a foreign entity is considered by Nevada to be immediately subject to state law, as if the entity had been formed in Nevada. The formation date for the newly domesticated entity will remain that of its original formation. Domestication in Nevada does not absolve a foreign entity of pre-existing obligations or liabilities incurred prior to its domestication, and conversely, upon domestication all of the rights, privileges and powers of the foreign entity, including assets and property, are deemed to be transferred to the newly domesticated entity.

The foreign entity also continues to exist in its original jurisdiction, even following a conversion. Nevada law views the newly domesticated company as a simple continuation of the foreign entity. In this situation, a foreign company must dissolve itself in its home jurisdiction separately, so as to avoid becoming subject to the laws of both its home jurisdiction and Nevada jurisdiction.

Tax Consequences

There is a saying that nothing ever comes for free, and this is largely true of converting business entities.

Converting a Corporation into an LLC: For tax purposes, the conversion of a Corporation into an LLC is treated as though the Corporation has liquidated itself, followed by a contribution of assets into the new LLC. The Corporation will realize a gain, being the difference between the fair market value of the Corporation over that of its assets. In addition, the individual shareholders will also realize a gain, based on the fair market value of their shareholdings over and above the value of the Corporation's assets. In the case of a Sub-Chapter S Corporation, the gain will be passed straight through to the shareholders, however in certain circumstances the Sub-Chapter S Corporation may also incur a built-in gains tax upon its liquidation. The gain realized may be capital or ordinary income depending on the nature of the assets transferred. Capital gains will be taxed at the capital gains rate, which is more favorable than ordinary income rates. The membership interests that each shareholder receives in the new LLC will be valued at the combined amount of their original shareholding plus applicable gains.

Merging a Corporation into an LLC: The same tax treatment set out above will be utilized when a Corporation and an LLC merge, leaving the LLC as the surviving entity. The Corporation will be considered liquidated, and capital gains will be incurred where the fair market value of the Corporation exceeds the value of its assets. Where an LLC is merged into a Corporation with the Corporation surviving, the LLC is deemed to have distributed its assets amongst its members, who then contribute those assets to the Corporation in return for stock. How much tax will be incurred will depend on the Operating Agreement and how taxes are passed through the LLC to its Members, but one thing is certain – someone will be paying something.

Converting a Partnership into an LLC: Due in part to existing similarities between the structure of partnerships and LLCs, conversion of one into another has fairly minimal tax consequences. As long as the amount of liabilities of a partnership does not exceed the amount of its assets, the transaction will be treated as tax-free. When an LLC is being treated as a partnership for tax purposes, the converted LLC entity may continue to use the old partnership's tax ID number, because as far as the IRS is concerned, it remains the same entity.

Bear in mind, however, that in a partnership, each partner is personally responsible for the debts of the partnership. Therefore, if a partnership converts to an LLC, this responsibility is removed, as the LLC provides limited liability protection for its members. What this means in tax terms, is that if you, as a limited partner, are ultimately responsible for the payment of $10,000 in debts of the partnership, and after the conversion into an LLC you are no longer personally liable for the repayment of that debt, the IRS will consider that you have gained $10,000 in taxable income, and tax you on it accordingly. This tax hit may be mitigated or reduced to an extent in a situation where creditors demand that limited partners sign personal guarantees over debts being transferred to a converted LLC, so that an element of personal responsibility remains. It is important when considering a conversion from a Limited Partnership to an LLC to ensure that the conversion is structured in such a way that the partners' liabilities remain the same, to avoid this tax hit.

Frequently Asked Questions

Can a conversion trigger dissenter's rights?

Yes, in some states members or partners may object to the conversion and demand to receive the fair value of their interest.

How is fair value determined?

Each state has its own procedure. In many cases an independent valuation is made which the dissenters may accept or reject in favor of their own appraisal. The end of the procedure involves a court deciding the fair market value of an interest.

How do creditors fare in a conversion?

Typically, all rights of creditors remain unimpaired and are assumed by the new entity.

What happens to existing contracts in a conversion?

Care must be taken to ensure that existing contracts, leases, licenses and other rights are not affected by a conversion. Agreements that are not assignable or transferable may be breached and lost if not handled properly.

What is unique about Wyoming's domestication process?

The State of Wyoming allows a foreign (non-Wyoming) entity to retain its original incorporation date upon domestication in Wyoming. So, if your California corporation was incorporated in 1955 and it is time to change states, you can domesticate in Wyoming and keep your 1955 incorporation date, which may provide credit and business continuity benefits for some.

Chapter Seventeen
Bankruptcy

There are times when things do not work out. It can be a result of the best intentions not fulfilled or a product of the black hearts of bad people in the business. For whatever reason, sometimes individuals and entities – LLCs and LPs included – must seek the assistance and protection from the United States Bankruptcy Courts.

Bankruptcy is a federal procedure for resolving and sorting out financial affairs. A Chapter 7 bankruptcy allows for the liquidation of a business. A Chapter 11 bankruptcy provides for the reorganization of a business. And a Chapter 13 bankruptcy handles the reorganization of an individual's affairs. Fortunately, there is no bankruptcy chapter providing for the liquidation of an individual. (Not that the credit card companies haven't thought of it.) It is also fortunate that debtors' prisons have been outlawed for over 150 years. Societies need to assist risk-takers, not punish them.

The bankruptcy courts are there to give people a fresh start. Bankruptcy procedure is also a section of law unto itself. It is a highly technical area of the law driven by local rules and judicial fiat – meaning that each court district and each judge within that district has their own way of doing things, and you'd better have a competent hometown bankruptcy attorney guide you through the maze. For if there was ever an area of unintended consequences ...

Case Number 12 - Dick, Edward and Sammy

As the three proprietors of an upscale men's clothing store, Dick, Edwards and Sammy have formed DES Men's, LLC to operate business. Dick is a self-centered person who, because he does not have a great deal of assets to bring into the business, is worried about control. Edward is an impressionable sort who is concerned about his welfare and who needs the business to work. Sammy just wants to see the business succeed. He is a team player and wants to see benefits for Dick and Edward as well as himself.

Dick, forever concerned about control, has directed his attorney to draft the Operating Agreement to provide that management control be held by the three members based on their membership ownership, with any change requiring unanimous consent of the interest holders. In this way, he can't be voted out of management control by the other two. Secure in his position, he begins to weave his web.

After several years, the store has grown in sales and customer base. To reach this level Sammy has taken a lower salary than Dick and Edward. He needs the money as much as they do but knows that sacrifices must be made. He is willing to make them. He ignores Dick's unnecessary business trips to Miami and aggressive entertainment deductions and continues to do what he feels is best for the business.

With the continued growth, the three decide they need a new retail location to complement the old downtown store. They also decide it is best to own the property rather than rent. So they form SED Properties, LLC (a separate LLC), to purchase a storefront property in a developing, upscale area. They obtain an SBA loan on the property but predictably the SBA requires a personal guarantee. They do not value the guarantees of Dick or Edward, who do not have the finest financial statements. Instead they insist upon the guarantee of Sammy, who is in a better financial position than his two partners. Always willing to help the team, Sammy signs the personal guarantee and agrees to manage the new location.

With Sammy out of the first store, Dick then starts talking to Edward about their partner. He insists that Sammy is cheating the company. Edward doesn't believe it at first. There is no evidence. But Dick continues to form his lie. And, as is often the case, a lie told often enough takes on a life of its own.

Sammy hears through the grapevine what Dick is saying about him. It offends him to the core. Here he has taken a lesser salary, guaranteed loans, gone out into the community to promote the business (unlike the others) and done everything he can to grow the business and Dick is assailing his integrity. Sammy becomes bitter and less concerned about the store's customers. Dick's lies are ruining his work.

Edward, always concerned about his own welfare, starts believing Dick. The new store's sales are falling off. Is Sammy stealing from the company? Something has to be done.

Dick has the answer. They will close down the new store. They will be free from the obligation to pay the high rent needed to pay the high mortgage to the SBA lender on the new property. Together, Dick and Edward, against Sammy's tremendous objections, vote to shut down the new store.

This leads to a chain of events that Dick has calculated but whose outcome was unforeseen.

The new store is not suited for anyone else. SED Properties, LLC, the new property-holding LLC, has spent a great deal of the SBA's money fixing it as an upscale men's store. It will not be rented any time soon. Dick and Edward, blaming Sammy for the new store's failure, refuse to have rent payments made from DES Men's LLC to SED properties, LLC. Being personally liable, Sammy makes the loan payments for several months but can't continue to do so. This leads to the SBA loan being put into default. While SED Properties, LLC, is the primary party responsible on the loan, the entity has no other assets besides the property. Dick and Edward threaten to bankrupt the entity. They don't need to, since SBA lenders take the easiest path toward collection. They go after Sammy, the personal guarantor of the loan, for the full defaulted loan amount. Sammy has no choice but to declare bankruptcy.

This is what Dick wanted all along. He knows the DES Men's LLC, Operating Agreement requires that a member who declares bankruptcy has to withdraw and be bought out at an artificially low value. Dick is overjoyed with Sammy's bankruptcy for it means the LLC can buy him out for $0.10 on the dollar and he can then own 50 percent of the LLC. In time he will find a way to bully out Edward and own the whole business.

But the bankruptcy laws get in the way of Dick's scheming.

While state laws may mandate dissolution upon the bankruptcy of a member, the bankruptcy courts do not have to follow those laws or the language of the Operating Agreement. Being federal courts, they pre-empt – or supercede – state laws. So, what Dick has angled for is not necessarily going to fly.

To understand why, look at it from the point of view of the bankruptcy court and the bankruptcy trustee assigned to administer each case, or bankruptcy estate. Their job is to resolve matters so that creditors can at least receive some return of money. Why would they allow Dick and Edward to purchase Sammy's one-third interest in DES Men's LLC, with a fair market value of $100,000 for $10,000? It is just not enough that the Operating Agreement calls for a $0.10 on the dollar buyout. The bankruptcy trustee can simply laugh at that provision as being void and against public policy.

In this case the trustee decides that the best way to benefit the estate is to keep the member's interest. Dick had originally directed that the Operating Agreement be drafted so that no one could take away the right of management from one holding a membership interest. This provision comes back to haunt him. The trustee steps into Sammy's shoes as a member and as a manager. He performs a forensic audit of the books and finds that Dick's business trips to Miami had no business purpose. He finds evidence of Dick's personal use of company credit cards. Dick's selfish and freewheeling ways are severely constrained by the trustee. Decisions are now to be made in the best interests of the business. If not, the trustee will simply go to the bankruptcy judge for a court order directing that such decision be made.

Dick and Edward can't handle the interference caused by the prudence of the bankruptcy trustee. Eventually, it is agreed that they will sell the company to the highest bidder. Dick's state law schemings are dashed by the federal power of the bankruptcy court.

In summary, when it comes to bankruptcy be careful what you wish for. While bankruptcy can provide a fresh start and is sometimes the only viable alternative for struggling entities, it can also lead to unexpected results and outcomes in certain cases.

Frequently Asked Questions

May an LLC or an LP apply for protection from creditors pursuant to the bankruptcy laws?

Yes, both can file under Chapter 7 (liquidation) and Chapter 11 (reorganization). A single-member LLC, as a disregarded tax entity, may be allowed to file an individual Chapter 13 reorganization. Be sure to check with a competent bankruptcy attorney regarding any of the issues discussed herein.

Is an LLC or an LP better in terms of bankruptcy protection?

An LP, because it has a general partner liable for debts of the entity, does not fare as well under bankruptcy procedure. Trustees will seek to hold general partners liable for certain obligations. Of course, using a limited liability entity such as a C Corporation or an LLC to serve as the general partner may minimize this consequence. Nevertheless, an LLC has no such corresponding personal liability.

Who has the authority to file a bankruptcy petition on behalf of an LLC or an LP?

In an LP, the general partner has this right. In an LLC, the Operating Agreement should set out this authority, whether it be the managers, or a unanimous or majority vote of the members.

May an LLC or LP be forced into bankruptcy?

Yes, involuntary bankruptcy proceedings can be brought against the entities.

Can a trustee sell the LLC/LP interest of a bankrupt member or partner?

Yes, while the operating or Partnership Agreement may have restrictions on transfer that may or may not be upheld, at the very least the trustee can sell an interest giving economic rights as an assignee, even if that interest does not offer full rights as a member or partner.

Chapter Eighteen
Special Situations – Divorce and Limited Liability Partnerships

Divorce

Case Number 13 – Dick and Patricia

With the money he receives from the sale of DES Men's, LLC, Dick and his wife, Patricia, buy a new retail business in a city 300 miles away. Dick is cocksure he can recreate the success enjoyed in his previous retail venture. He runs the new business through a new LLC owned equally by himself and his wife.

But things don't work out. The new city is not used to Dick's style and tastes. With the business suffering, so does the marriage. Soon Dick and Patricia are talking about divorce. A property settlement is worked out whereby Dick gives up his half of the new LLC to Patricia. He agrees to be personally responsible for half of the existing debts, including some Form 941 federal payroll tax liabilities.

Patricia feels she could make a go of the business with Dick out of the way. Dick receives their home in their original city and moves back. The divorce is finalized. Unfortunately, Patricia can't make a go of the business. Dick has turned off quite a few customers and their word of mouth is bad. She can't meet the obligations and asks Dick to contribute money as he has promised. Dick's response is to file bankruptcy, leaving his ex-wife Patricia responsible for 100 percent of the debts, as well as a failing business.

As is indicated, LLC and LP assets are property interests to be dealt with in a divorce proceeding. If the parties can't agree on how to split up their assts, a judge will decide. If a judge has to decide, the parties are going to split more with their attorneys than they will amongst themselves. For certain bitter contestants in a divorce battle, that is just fine.

In certain divorce actions the issues of which spouse is the manager/partner and which one holds the voting rights will be very important. As well, the entity's taxation as a Corporation or a Partnership (which may tend to deflate or inflate true entity cashflow) will be a significant factor in determining alimony and child support calculations and equitable distributions. A good divorce attorney will appreciate these considerations.

In our case involving Patricia, there are two points of concern.

First, be careful of what LLC, LP or other entity assets you accept in a settlement. As with Patricia, she accepted the short end of the settlement. She thought Dick would be obligated to pay half the liabilities. She never thought he would go bankrupt to avoid his responsibilities. What a guy.

Unfortunately, this scenario occurs far too often.

Second, as partners/members of an LP/LLC with combative or concerning spouses you may want to consider a separate buy-sell agreement or a provision in the Partnership or Operating Agreement to deal with the issue of divorce. A well-drafted agreement signed by both spouses and reviewed by their separate counsel can give the entity the right to buy either spouse's interest in the event of divorce. That way the entity will never have to deal with the possibility that a property settlement will transfer to a non-welcome spouse an interest in the business.

The last thing the other members/partners want is a disruptive, vindictive, know-nothing spouse telling them how to run their business so he or she can keep up the monthly payment expectations. The money to buy out such a spouse pursuant to a pre-arranged agreement is money well spent.

Limited Liability Partnerships

A Limited Liability Partnership (LLP) is a method by which a General Partnership is registered with a state in order to minimize the joint and several liability of the general partners. In some states this is known as a Registered LLP, or RLLP. When a Limited Partnership so registers in some states to limit the liability of its general partners, a Limited Liability Limited Partnership, or LLLP, is registered. Upon filing, the LLP or LLLP retains its taxable status as a partnership and retains its existing legal identity.

While approved in all 50 states, New York, Nevada, Oregon, California and certain other states only allow LLPs to be conducted by professional firms (lawyers, accountants, doctors and the like).

The difference between an LLP and an LLC or LP is that in an LLP you are attempting to direct responsibility for all acts of general partners to just the general partner that made the mistake. In an accounting firm, for example, the auditor who missteps will be solely responsible in an LLP, and not the other partners who did not work on the file. In an LLC or LP setting the entity itself could be held liable for the mistakes of its employees. In a professional setting involving possible malpractice claims not all the other partners want to take on that potential liability. They would rather each partner be responsible for their own mistakes, which can be accomplished with an LLP.

Another reason LLPs are used is that certain states do not allow professionals or others to practice through an LLC. Certain states such as California also heavily tax LLCs, which may make an LLP more attractive. But beware. An LLP is not the same as a professional corporation. In some states, LLPs have unlimited liability for loans, leases and the like, even when not personally guaranteed by the partners.

This general discussion is conditioned by the fact that each state's law is different. Be sure to consult with your professional advisor before proceeding.

Chapter Nineteen
Comprehensive Strategies Made Easy

Case Number 14 - Emily and Joel; Sarah and Scott

Emily and Joel are husband and wife, as are Sarah and Scott. Emily and Sarah are twin sisters and have worked very successfully together before. The four of them have come up with a business for the efficient placement of online advertising. They know the Internet is going to be a valuable business tool in the future. They know that, as with the steel and automobile industries in prior decades, the dot-com shakeout is just a part of the normal business cycle. The Internet is going to make those with solid business fundamentals and judgment a great deal of money. Now, as they are starting their business, they needed to structure it to accomplish their future goals.

The two couples each have three children. They know the strategies of gifting for estate planning purposes and want to be certain that their structure allows for such a strategy.

They have developed valuable intellectual property – patents and trademarks involving their Online ABC System – and want to protect it as best they can. The structure has to include such a protection.

They have learned of the advantages of C Corporations by reading *Own Your Own Corporation* and want to receive the maximum medical and retirement benefits allowable. At the same time, they want a flow-through entity for tax purposes. But they know they can't use a Sub-Chapter S Corporation, because some day they may need to give up equity to a Canadian partner in Toronto, which is not allowed in a Sub-Chapter S Corporation.

They have also learned that to hold assets and equipment in a separate entity can provide asset protection to the parent entity. If the parent entity is sued there will be fewer assets for a creditor to reach because they are leased from a separate, independent entity. In the same vein, they have learned that money can be loaned from a separate LLC entity to the parent entity. The loan can be reflected by a promissory note and security agreement with the parent's assets secured by a UCC-1 financing statement. They know that the advantage with such a strategy is two-fold:

First, they can have their principal paid back with interest on the monies used to advance the business. Instead of contributing money directly to the parent entity and having it tied up as equity, they can have the monies loaned be paid back as a debt obligation from the borrowing LLC.

Second, because the debt is secured by a UCC-1 financing statement on the parent entity's assts (those few remaining ones that aren't already leased from the leasing LLC) the covered assets are encumbered for purposes of a later creditor. That is, a later creditor cannot reach the assets because the loaning entity has first right to them through the security agreement and UCC-1 financing statement.

They also know that their business would own the office building they work out of but that it is better to put it into a separate LLC for asset protection purposes. In this way, the parent entity can lease from the real estate entity, thus making all the mortgage payments and, if the local market justified it, some extra money for the owners. And again, if the parent entity is sued the real estate will be protected from attack.

So they meet with their attorney and accountant who come up with the following, somewhat intimidating, structure:

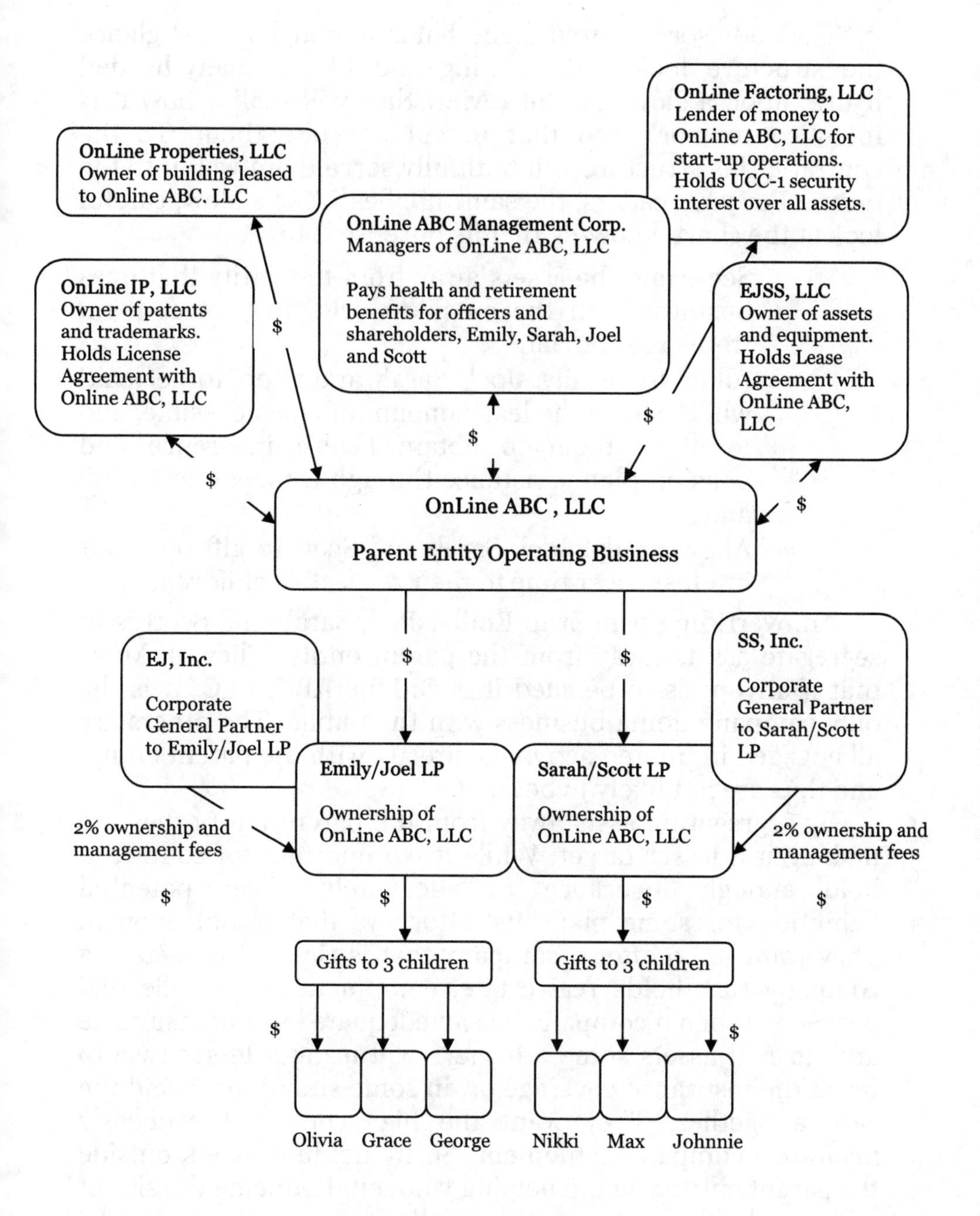
OnLine Factoring, LLC
Lender of money to OnLine ABC, LLC for start-up operations. Holds UCC-1 security interest over all assets.
OnLine Properties, LLC
Owner of building leased to Online ABC. LLC
OnLine ABC Management Corp.
Managers of OnLine ABC, LLC
Pays health and retirement benefits for officers and shareholders, Emily, Sarah, Joel and Scott
OnLine IP, LLC
Owner of patents and trademarks. Holds License Agreement with Online ABC, LLC
EJSS, LLC
Owner of assets and equipment. Holds Lease Agreement with OnLine ABC, LLC
$
OnLine ABC , LLC
Parent Entity Operating Business
EJ, Inc.
Corporate General Partner to Emily/Joel LP
SS, Inc.
Corporate General Partner to Sarah/Scott LP
Emily/Joel LP
Ownership of OnLine ABC, LLC
Sarah/Scott LP
Ownership of OnLine ABC, LLC
2% ownership and management fees
2% ownership and management fees
Gifts to 3 children
Gifts to 3 children
Olivia
Grace
George
Nikki
Max
Johnnie

Their advisors assured them that at although at first glance the structure looks intimidating and like a many-headed hydra, upon a slow, careful review they will realize how it is intended to work and that it will not bite them. To the contrary, this structure will faithfully serve them well into the future. For you readers, the same applies. Take a slow, careful look at the chart, knowing that its purpose is to:

- Segregate the assets away from the entity that does business with the outside world, to protect them from creditor claims;
- Allow for Emily, Joel, Sarah and Scott to get paid while paying the least amount of taxes possible, and to allow them to obtain health insurance and pension plan assistance through a corporate entity; and
- Allow Emily, Joel, Sarah and Scott to gift out their interests over time to their respective children.

An overriding benefit to Emily, Joel, Sarah and Scott is to segregate assets away from the parent entity. They all know that if anyone is to be sued it is OnLine ABC, LLC. It is the only company doing business with the public. The others are all engaged in limited activities directly with the parent entity, and thus are not likely to be sued.

By segregating assts away from the parent entity they are making it a lesser target. While it is important, of course, to hold enough insurance to adequately cover potential liabilities, for some plaintiffs' attorneys that is not enough. They want to go after a company that is rich with assets – a company that holds real estate, equipment and intellectual property. When a company has an adequate level of insurance and no real assets some attorneys will bring a lesser case to reach the insurance coverage or, in some situations, avoid the case altogether. They want the big score, not a measly insurance company settlement. So by holding assets outside the parent entity you are helping yourself. Reducing the size of a big red bull's-eye to a much smaller target is always a good strategy.

Another benefit to the structure is the management Corporation. By having OnLine ABC Management Corp. serve as manager of OnLine ABC, LLC, monies can flow from the LLC to a C Corporation for services rendered. This money can then be used for all the benefits afforded a C Corporation – health plans, retirement plans, educational awards and the like. In addition, by paying salaries and federal employment taxes through OnLine ABC Management Corp., the threat of C Corporation double-taxation is minimized. Through proper planning and the payment of salaries and related benefits, OnLine ABC Management Corp. will never show much of a profit and will never pay dividends to its shareholders. So they will never be taxed twice on the same income.

By paying the statutory amount of federal employment taxes through the C Corporation they will also be free to receive income from other sources in the structure without paying the 15.3 percent in employment taxes. It should be noted that income from other sources will still be subject to the 2.9 percent Medicare tax, which has no statutory minimum level. But the receipt of income from the other LLCs free of the 15.3 percent in employment taxes is a significant increase in flow-through benefits.

Another advantage to the structure is that money can flow through the parent LLC to each LP. From each LP it flows to each limited partner, which through gifting are Emily and Joel and Sarah and Scott's children. The advisors indicate that children over 14 pay a much lower tax than adults. For example, on income of $1,500 at the top tax rate adults pay over $500 in taxes, whereas children over 14 years pay just a little over $100. By income shifting, the parents can benefit their children with some savings for later productive uses.

The advisors explain that gifting to the children can flexibly occur in each one of the entities on the chart. Emily and Joel are free to gift their interests in Online ABC, LLC to Olivia, Grace and George in one year and EJSS, LLC in the next year. If Sarah and Scott feel that the real estate in OnLine Properties, LLC is going to go up in value in the next few years they are free to focus on gifting those interests to Nikki, Max and Johnnie for as long as they can gift it out.

The advisors also indicate that some of the LLCs should be located in Nevada and some in Wyoming. There are a number of reasons for this. First, Nevada and Wyoming laws are very protective of LLC members. The Nevada and Wyoming legislatures have made charging orders the exclusive remedy a creditor has against an LLC, whereas in California, the courts will allow a creditor to reach right into an LLC to pull out assets. The Nevada and Wyoming legislatures have dictated that this will not happen. Instead, a creditor must now stand in the shoes of a limited partner or member and wait for distributions. As discussed, this is a powerful deterrent to frivolous litigation. Also, by spreading the LLCs between two different state locations, they are creating the appearance of roadblocks. A plaintiff's attorney looking to sue realizes that he or she must travel to, or retain, attorneys in two different states. The more problems that Emily, Joel, Sarah and Scott could create for such people, the better.

A second Nevada and Wyoming advantage is that there are no state taxes on income received into an LLC or LP. By organizing the entities in Nevada and Wyoming, which both also feature very affordable filing fees, monies can be received without paying any additional taxes. Of course, if the owners of the LLC are residents of a high-tax state such as California or New York, the income flowing through the LLC will flow right back onto their personal tax return, forcing the payment of state income taxes.

The solution to this issue has three alternatives. If you like living on the beach at Malibu or the energy of the Upper West Side in New York City or the comforts and familiarity of wherever you live, you simply may want to pay the state taxes. There are costs associated with the privilege of living in desirable areas and sometimes high state (and, in New York City, local) taxes are one of them. You may decide to use a Nevada or Wyoming LLC for the asset protection benefits they offer and continue to pay your home state's taxes on the income. If you do, at least you can always justify the business expense of a trip to Lake Tahoe or Jackson Hole.

A second alternative is to have the LLC be owned by a C Corporation. Subject to the controlled group status and accumulated earnings tax rules, money may flow into an LLC and be passed onto a Nevada or Wyoming C Corporation. There, the first $50,000 in income is taxed at only 15 percent on the federal level. And there is no tax at the Nevada or Wyoming state level. Monies can again be used for retirement plans and health benefits, subject to overall limits within the entire structure. Also, by using a nominee officer and director, your involvement in the entity can be shielded from view. It is important to note that if called into court and under oath, you must answer truthfully about your ownership of an entity. But by using nominees – persons other than yourself – to serve as officers, directors, manager and general partners, your name may be kept off the public record as to your involvement. This in turn may prevent you from ever being called in the first place to testify. Our associate, Altacian Corporate Services, offers a nominee service for $650 per year. For many, it is money well spent.

A third alternative to paying high state income taxes on monies flowing through the LLC is to move to Nevada, Wyoming, or another no-tax state. In my practice I have had numerous clients move to Nevada for just that reason. Once they arrive they enjoy the quality of life benefits, but the motivation to move was strictly taxes. Lake Tahoe has thousands of residents who are tax refugees. And, there are as many people who have set up Nevada structures with the intent of moving to Nevada in the future. They will pay state taxes on flow-through income now, but when they move, their Nevada entities will be in place, and their tax situation will be greatly improved.

It should be noted that OnLine Properties, LLC, which owns real estate leased to the parent company, and EJSS, LLC, which owns assets and equipment leased to the parent company, will be considered to be doing business in the state of the parent company. They are engaged in a trade or business, the leasing of real property and equipment, into the parent company's home state. As such, they must register as a Nevada (or foreign) LLC doing business in the home state and may have to pay state taxes on the income generated. There is really no way around this situation short of moving the parent company to Nevada, Wyoming or another no-tax state.

Nevertheless, OnLine IP, LLC and OnLine Factoring, LLC may not be considered to be doing business in the parent company's home state, since the intellectual property and loans are generated from either Nevada or Wyoming. Subject to the Geoffrey case we discussed in Chapter Eleven, the patents and trademarks licensed from the holding LLC to the operating LLC will be expenses to the parent and gain to the intellectual property LLC in Nevada. The same is true for the factoring LLC, which has loaned money through an entity based in Nevada. Please note that it is wise and suggested to have such Nevada entities set up and use a Nevada bank account and have their tax returns prepared by a Nevada accountant. You want to carry forward the incidences of a Nevada presence, and bank accounts and tax preparation in Nevada are an excellent way to do so. Also, a Nevada or Wyoming office presence with a phone, web site and office address is frequently a good strategy. Our affiliate, Altacian Corporate Services, offers a comprehensive office package for both Nevada and Wyoming entities at competitive prices. You may call toll-free to 1-800-785-9811 to receive additional information on this service.

In summary, the entire strategy works well for Emily, Joel, Sarah and Scott, as well as their children. Their important assets are protected, they are able to achieve maximum benefits through their C Corporation and maximum flow-through of income through their other entities. They are able to gift assets to their children at a discount and provide for their future security. And they have achieved their overall objective: to successfully protect and grow their assets.

Conclusion

You have now learned a great deal about the strategies used by the rich to protect and grow their assets. You have also learned the mechanics for operating an LLC and LP in order to further protect yourself and your family.

The strategies and operational knowledge you have gained are both powerful and beneficial. Use them to your maximum advantage to protect and grow your assets. Use them to benefit you and your loved ones into the future.

Good luck.

About the Author

Garrett Sutton, Esq., author of *Own Your Own Corporation* and *How to Buy and Sell a Business* in the Rich Dad's Advisors series, is an attorney with over twenty years experience in assisting individuals and businesses to determine their appropriate corporate structure, limit their liability, protect their assets and advance their financial and personal goals.

Garrett and his law firm, Sutton Law Center, is based in Reno, Nevada, and represents hundreds of corporations, limited liability companies, limited partnerships and individuals in their business-related law matters, including incorporations, contracts, mergers and acquisitions and ongoing business-related legal advice.

Garrett attended Colorado College and the University of California at Berkeley, where he received a B.S. in Business Administration in 1975. He graduated with a J.D. in 1978 from Hastings College of Law, the University of California's law school in San Francisco. He has appeared in the *Wall Street Journal* and other publications. He is the host of the SuccessDNA Radio Hour, found archived at www.successdna.com.

Garrett is a member of the State Bar of Nevada, the State Bar of California, and the American Bar Association. He has written numerous professional articles and has served on the Publication Committee of the State Bar of Nevada.

Garrett enjoys speaking with entrepreneurs on the advantages of forming business entities. He is a frequent lecturer for the Nevada Microenterprise Institute, the Small Business Administration and the Rich Dad's Advisors series.

Garrett serves on the boards of the American Baseball Foundation, located in Birmingham, Alabama, and the Reno-Nevada-based Sierra Kids Foundation.

For more information on Garrett Sutton and Sutton Law Center, please visit his website at www.sutlaw.com.

Where Can I Receive More Free Entrepreneur Information?

Sign up to receive SuccessDNA's FREE e-newsletter, which features informative articles and entrepreneur resources. Visit www.successdna.com for more details.

How Can I Protect My Personal and Business Assets?

For information on forming corporations, limited liability companies and limited partnerships to protect your personal and business holdings in all 50 states, as well as useful tips and strategies, visit Altacian Corporate Services, Inc.'s web site, located at www.altacian.com, or call toll-free 1-800-785-9811.

Special Offer – Mention this book and receive a 5 percent discount on the basic formation fee.

SuccessDNA Publications

Order Here to Receive our Quality Business and Financial Books

ABCs for CEOs, written by Jet Parker, discusses the 26 key skills every business leader must possess.

The Cave Creed, written by Frank Troppe, discusses the importance of Competence, Agreement, Vigor and Execution in employment relationships.

Design/Build Your Business, written by Ron Sacchi, provides the blueprints for starting and succeeding in business.

Get Off the Couch!, written by Kenji Sax, Ph.D., shows how to use psychology for success in Business.

The Healthy Executive, written by Amy Sutton, is a complete explanation and method for attaining and maintaining your most important asset, your physical health. Topics from diet to exercise are presented in an easy-to-read and practical manner.

Order Form

Please send me:

___ *ABCs for CEOs* at $19.95 each
___ *The Cave Creed* at $19.95 each
___ *Design/Build Your Business* at $24.95 each
___ *Get Off the Couch!* at $17.95 each
___ *The Healthy Executive* at $19.95 each
___ *How to Use Limited Liability Companies & Limited Partnerships* at $19.95 each

Please add $6.95 shipping and handling per order (NV residents please add 7.375% sales tax). Shipping on 3 or more books is free. Non-US orders must be accompanied by a money order in US funds. Allow 15 days for delivery.

My check or money order for $_________ is enclosed.

Please charge my ☐ VISA ☐ MasterCard ☐ American Express

Name: ____

Address: ____

City/State/Zip: _______________________________________

Phone: ______________________ Email: _____________________

Card # _____________________________ Exp Date: ___________

Signature: ____

Please make your check or money order payable and return to:
SuccessDNA Inc. ♦ PO Box 1450 ♦ Verdi, NV 89439
To order by credit card, call 1-800-293-7411 or fax to 1-775-824-0105
Also visit www.successdna.com to order books, tapes and other materials or to sign up for our e-newsletter!

NOTES

NOTES

NOTES

NOTES

NOTES

NOTES